Be Still

Uncovering God's Solution for Achieving Happiness, Healing, and Wholeness

Anita Marchesani, PhD

Note to reader: All names and identifying information about some of the people mentioned in this book have been altered to protect their privacy.

BE STILL: UNCOVERING GOD'S SOLUTION FOR ACHIEVING HAPPINESS, HEALING, AND WHOLENESS.

This book is dedicated to my personal Lord and Savior, Jesus Christ. I am forever grateful for His work in my life, and not giving up on pursuing my heart.

I could never accomplish anything in my life without my supportive, beautiful family.

Thank you, Frank, for so many incredibly wonderful years of marriage, and for always supporting my "crazy" ideas.

To Lucas and Alex – I love you more than I can possibly convey in words.

Mom and Dad – you could not have been more supportive and loving.

Finally, thank you, Yahweh, for the incredible blessings You have bestowed in my life, even when I was far from You.

Prologue

Be still, and know that I am God.
I will be exalted among the nations,
I will be exalted in the earth!
Psalm 46:10 NKJV

These people draw near to Me with their mouth, And honor Me with their lips, but their heart is far from me.
 Matthew 15:8 NKJV

INTRODUCTION

"I'm just so tired of dealing with all of this!"

Anna sat across from me, hunched over in a position reflecting the weight of the emotional burden she had been carrying for most of her 42 years on this earth. She held a tissue tightly in one hand and methodically picked apart pieces of it with the other, letting the ripped paper fall gently to the ground. I would pick it up after she left my office.

"When will God take this from me? When will He break this crushing depression and anger?" A distant cousin had molested Anna when they attended a family reunion when Anna was 6 years old. That was the only time she had been abused as a child, but it only takes one time for evil to insert lies and distortions into the human soul. After her cousin molested her, he left her in a small closet in a building at the park where the reunion was held. On his way out of the room, he turned and dismissively told her, "You won't tell anyone about this because now you're dirty and used up. No one would believe someone like you, anyway. You're useless."

Anna had sought therapy many times during her teenage and young adult years. Because of the impact of her childhood abuse, she developed chronic anxiety that made her withdraw from meeting life's challenges, under-achieve in her career, and plagued her with self-doubt and fear in her marriage. Usually, the therapy helped take the edge off her emotional pain, giving her enough strength to keep going for a year or two. Then she would find herself needing therapy again to address the same stuff that just kept repeatedly arising. Each time, she thought she dealt with it, but it was an illusion – healing never really happened. Anna got just enough of a boost to hide the pain a little longer.

By the time she came to me, Anna was depressed. She was despondent over realizing that, despite all her hard work in therapy over the years, it seemed nothing really changed. She still coped with periods of intense overwhelm and stress, and then it would morph into helplessness. Anna was sick of dealing with this. And so was her husband, who was losing patience with her as each year passed by. She was referred to me by a family friend who knew I had a process to work with emotionally wounded people by fusing the healing power of Jesus Christ with clinical psychology.

"Anna, when you pray, what does God tell you?" I asked. She responded in a way that many people respond – with Bible verses:

"He says that I can do all things through Christ, who strengthens me. And that He will never leave me or forsake me," Anna responded, with her perfectly rehearsed verses meant to combat the bone-rattling things she *actually* believed about herself – that she was unlovable, dirty, and worthless.

The problem was that Anna was a "good Christian," raised in a "good Christian home." She memorized and recited Bible verses to encourage her each day. She honored God with her lips. However, she did not believe these verses to be true, or at least true for her. She wanted them to be true and reciting them renewed her hope that they would somehow finally sink in and take root inside her soul.

Deep down in the very core of her being, Anna failed to believe what God said about her. Instead, she believed what the spiritual enemy said about her. Blessedly, God has given us a solution to bridge this seemingly canyon-sized gap between knowing Scripture in our minds but not believing it in our hearts. Anna received the healing she desperately needed but would never find in traditional counseling.

Anna knew in her brain what God believes about her – she was skilled at memorizing Bible verses but believed the complete opposite about herself in her heart. She needed to close that gap. Anna needed to somehow translate the truth of who God says she is from her brain down into her heart.

This is the crucial level of healing that never happened during previous therapy sessions. Some emotional wounds cut so deep that only a supernatural encounter with God Almighty Himself can convince a person that the lies they believe are, in fact, *lies*. Secular therapists will never invite God into a therapy session, although it is the only thing that can help.

That was going to change on this particular day.

"Anna, what is it you want from God?" I asked her, intending to direct her attention away from reliving her daily pain and instead toward a solution.

"Well, I want Him to take away my pain. I was hurt so badly that day; that boy branded me for the rest of my life. I can't have a fulfilling relationship with my husband, I know I'm angrier with my kids than I have to be, and I just can't get out of bed in the mornings......" Anna continued with the long list of how devastated her life has been since that fateful day. But she never answered my question – she still did not articulate what she wanted from God. I think she did not even know what she wanted or needed because she had spent so much of her life rehearsing and reliving her pain.

It was time to interrupt her. Repeating pain over and over again is damaging and only "legitimizes" and solidifies the lies she believed about herself. There was too much mental chatter going on in her head and I was getting access to it via her lengthy explanations. I had to take firmer control of the session and lead Anna to quiet her mind.

"ANNA! Stop talking and look at me!" I said emphatically, knowing I was coming across as borderline rude.

Slightly shocked, Anna lifted her head and met my gaze. As most people in pain do, she looked away rather quickly. Steadily looking at another person in the eyes can be quite intense. It forces both people's attention to the present moment, rather than continuing to talk about the past and how it makes us feel. It forces the people involved to *be still*. That feels intimidating to someone who keeps their minds active to avoid silence and stillness. Mental chatter prevents us from thinking about painful things.

When she started to look away, I said, "No, Anna, LOOK at me and keep looking at me."

This time, she met my eyes and stared at me for a few seconds. Once I knew she was "locked into me" and no longer thinking about her past, I asked, "Anna, can we go into prayer right now and ask God what He thinks?"

She nodded her head yes, sniffled a bit, and then closed her eyes and bowed her head as I prayed:

> Heavenly Father, the Maker of heaven and earth, the grand Creator, the One who knew Anna before You established the foundation of the earth, who knows the end from the beginning, who loves Anna with an everlasting love and has Anna's name written on the palm of Your hand – Father, this is your daughter. She is Your princess. She is Your heir. And she is hurting deeply. She has come to believe lies about

herself – that she is dirty and unlovable. She knows they are lies, but Father, they *feel* true to her. Lord God, please speak to Anna right now and tell her what You want her to know about this situation."

Then, we sat in still silence. After about five or six seconds, Anna started to weep again. But this weeping had a different quality to it. I knew she was crying from release and relief, not from pain and agony anymore.

"Anna, what did God say to you?" I asked, knowing with 100 percent certainty that God had just spoken directly, intimately, and personally to Anna. He always shows up when people learn to be still and pray like this.

Gathering herself together, and with a sense of semi-bewilderment, Anna said, "He told me He loves me and that I belong to Him." She gave a watery smile and a short chuckle. Again, Anna started to cry, but with tears of joy and belonging, with tears of knowing the truth and having her lies corrected, replaced, and permanently healed.

I reached over to hug her, tears filling my own eyes at one of the most beautiful experiences in the world – watching the exact moment of true, intense, deep, and personal healing after hearing an intimate word from God Himself. This is a privilege every time I have the honor of working with someone in this way.

But Anna never would have heard from God as long as she insisted on mental busyness and chatter. Accepting stillness, as we are all commanded, allows us to know He is God. He is sovereign and in control, even when we feel out of control.

The Healing Power of Biblical Stillness

I want to introduce you to a concept that is not new or revolutionary: stillness. It is simple and profound; indeed, it is the key to unlocking the healing that God promises us in Scripture, the healing and relief to which we have access through His Son, Jesus Christ, and His finished work on the cross.

This book will delve into emotional pain – where it comes from, why it sticks around, how it impacts us, and, of course, how we can learn to allow healing from God. The central feature involves this idea that God tells us is so important – stillness.

When I use the word "still" or "stillness," I refer primarily to *mental* stillness. When you hear the term "stillness," you may immediately think of being *physically* still. I would imagine God wants us to do that too! In fact, in many places in His Word, he tells us to "stand strong," to "stand" or to "be steadfast." This indicates a position of power but not of action.

Emotional stillness also puts us in this same position. Stillness is powerful because it demands that we restrain our own action. It forces us to dial back our own striving tendencies and allow God to go first and act on our behalf. If we insist on motion – whether physical or mental/emotional chatter – then we crowd out God.

Sometimes people need to achieve physical stillness in order to facilitate emotional and mental stillness. It is important to always keep in mind that being physically still does not automatically mean you are mentally still. In fact, most of us are experts at maintaining mental activity, chatter, and clutter when we lay down to try to sleep at night. We are physically still in bed, but our minds keep going.

Mental stillness can feel like an elusive goal. But I promise that as you read this book and understand how powerful God says stillness is, you will learn how to increase stillness in your mind. Stillness is so powerful, in fact, that it is the only position in which we can place ourselves to receive God's emotionally healing words through the Holy Spirit.

While you may be eager to learn more about this concept and know the steps of how all of this works, part of you may also consider this a scary topic. After all, you have spent a lifetime carefully crafting ways of managing your emotional pain and stresses. Upsetting your emotional balancing act by doing the one thing that practically guarantees you will connect with painful wounds might make you want to run for the proverbial hills.

I urge you to stick with this book! God wants you to be healed. He would not have sent His Son to live, be brutally tortured, die, and then conquer death for you if this were not true. Consider what Jesus declared in Luke 4:18b (NKJV) as a fulfillment of a prophecy in Isaiah: "He has sent Me to heal the brokenhearted."

This is a promise directly from God Himself. What God promises, He will fulfill: "God is not a man, that He should lie, Nor a son of man, that He should repent. Has He said, and will He not do? Or has He spoken, and will He not make it good?" (Num 23:19).

Maybe you feel like Anna felt. Maybe at times you even feel worse. Emotional struggles hinder us. They keep us psychologically crippled. Just like a physical injury hampers our ability to move and function properly, emotional injury – in the form of childhood wounds, hurts, abuse, or tension-filled households – keeps us from moving forward in the will and purpose that God has established for us.

We keep ourselves distracted just trying to make it through the day. We use huge quantities of mental energy protecting our hearts from being hurt again. We "live small" because we have come to believe that we are nobody special, we are useless, we are unimportant, we are unlovable, and maybe even invisible. It is these false beliefs that form the wounds on our hearts. Those old wounds have a profound impact on what you choose to do every single day.

Connecting with even a portion of that wound may sound about as tempting as a root canal. But I promise if you mindfully and prayerfully make your way through this book, understand why you have your struggles, and why they do not disappear so easily, you will feel more empowered and equipped to claim God's healing through stilling your mind.

Chapter One: The Epidemic of Emotional Pain

According to the Centers for Disease Control, over one in twenty Americans over the age of 12 experience an episode of depression (meaning it lasts for at least two weeks) at least once in a one-year period. Some research shows it affects around 19 million adults each year. These statistics do not even include children.

Anxiety is the largest mental health problem in the United States. According to the Anxiety and Depression Association of America (ADAA https://adaa.org/about-adaa/press-room/facts-statistics), a whopping 40 *million* adults over the age of 18 experience an anxiety disorder. That represents over 18% of the adult population in our country.

These numbers are growing and expanding into some concerning and alarming territory. The rate of suicide is skyrocketing and has now moved into the 10th leading cause of death in the nation. Most alarmingly, between 2017 and 2015, the number of children aged 5 to 18 presenting to emergency rooms with suicidal thoughts and attempts have doubled. Let me repeat that statistic: the number of suicidal children in the United States of America has *doubled* in less than ten years. If that does not grab your attention, perhaps this piece of data will: The average age of the children at the emergency room for wanting to commit suicide is 13 years old! And 43% of those children are between the ages of 5 and 11. If this does not wake people up to the realities of spiritual decline, and the results of removing God from society, I am not sure what will.

Drug use and overdose problems plague our communities and cost Americans $740 billion each year, according to the National Institute on Drug Abuse. Another study showed Americans reported substantially higher levels of depressive symptoms in the years between 2000 – 2010 than in the decade from 1980 through 1990.[1]Unprecedented numbers of people are dying from their attempts to fill a spiritual and emotional void.

You may have to take a deep breath before you read this next startling piece of data: In 1999, just under 20,000 Americans died from drug overdoses. In 2017 (the year for which the most recent data was available at the time of writing this book), more than 72,000 people died from a drug overdose! I am practically crying while typing this – my heart breaks for the tens of thousands of families who grieve and mourn for their loved ones who died in such painful ways. This reflects a two-fold increase in the number of deaths due to overdose in just ten years.

As a society, we are not heading in the right direction. Levels of stress and overwhelm zoomed upward around 2010 and remain at consistently high and disturbing, rates (APA Stress in America). Our teens report staggering rates of loneliness, despite being "connected" via social media. But it's not just our teenagers and young people who feel disconnected – adults at all ages do too. According to a recent Cigna survey, American adults experience loneliness at "epidemic levels.

I will not continue with the discouraging data, as I trust that the message has been delivered – despite all the modern medicine, well established and well-studied psychotherapy techniques, and the expansion of access to mental health and addiction treatments, we are getting *worse*!

Couple this highly troubling situation with the reported decrease in church attendance and I think we can more fully understand why our nation is so emotionally unhealthy. I hesitate to discuss church attendance because I believe it is not an adequate metric to measure how many people are being saved by yielding their hearts to Christ each year. With the dramatic rise in home and micro churches, plus the growth of small groups and individual Bible studies in communities that are not attached to a specific church, I think we stand on the edge of the next Great Awakening. I wish I could substantiate my "hunch" with data and facts, but I

---

[1] Time Period and Birth Cohort Differences in Depressive Symptoms in the US, 1982-2013 (SpringerLink – Jean M. Twenge)

cannot. Perhaps you have the same inkling about the movement of God right now?

When people struggle to such a degree, and with the removal and marginalization of God in society over the past 40 years, the Holy Spirit moves people to find the one thing that can truly heal, restore, and repair: the power of Jesus Christ.

The problem we, as Christ followers, face in ministering to unbelievers (or even to new Christians) is that we, ourselves, are the walking wounded. We "should" be the model of the health, healing, and wholeness available in Christ. We "should" be walking in freedom and victory, proclaiming our testimonies of deliverance from oppressive mental conditions at every opportunity. But that does not happen, does it? Why do Christians struggle with healing just like unbelievers do? And why would unbelievers yield their hearts to a savior who we "say" will heal and restore….but has not done it for us?

If Christ was sent by God to "…heal the brokenhearted, to proclaim liberty to the captives And recovery of sight to the blind, To set at liberty those who are oppressed" (Luke 4:18), what happened? Certainly, we hear stories and testimonies from various ministries – praise God! But shouldn't we hear these stories constantly? Admittedly, I issue my opinion without numbers or facts behind it, but it seems only a small percentage of Christians experience these healings that are promised to us throughout Scripture.

Why is this? While I have no answer, I do know that, from this moment onward, you can dedicate the rest of your life to claiming that victory over emotional pain that is *promised* you in Scripture. It is my deepest prayer that taking this first step of learning how to "be still" will vault you to new levels in your relationship with God and into the promises He has for you.

Why would God heal us? I want to answer this question by first painting a picture of what happens when we maintain and carry around our emotional wounds. When we are depressed, discouraged, nervous, worried, and anxious, how productive are we?

I definitely do not operate at my highest levels when I feel overwhelmed by emotional hurt and pain. And neither do most people. In fact, depressed people often have trouble simply getting out of bed in the morning, and they lack the motivation to initiate activities and to generally participate in life. Anxious people spend most of their energies trying to avoid situations that provoke their worry and fears, so they don't go to social functions, they resist assignments at work that requires them to do anxiety-producing tasks like public speaking, and they don't volunteer in their churches and communities because they are easily intimidated by leadership positions.

People with deep emotional wounds also have problems in their personal relationships. The baggage we bring from childhood (and none of us escapes childhood unscathed, FYI) plays out in the close relationships we have in the current day. If your parents abused you, neglected you, or generally did a lousy job of meeting your needs, you carry wounds on your heart that impact what you believe about people and how they treat you. If you grew up feeling unloved, you will mistakenly believe you are unlovable. Or you may deep down believe that you cannot trust anyone and that you are at high risk for being hurt, betrayed, or let down. You might believe in your heart that you are dirty and no one could possibly love the "real you," so you work very hard to create, project, and maintain an image of the "good girl/boy."

Now, please understand that these beliefs we carry with us from childhood are relatively subconscious. For the most part, we are unaware of our deepest levels of emotional hurts, let alone examining how they impact the way we show up in relationships. You will learn more in chapter six about how this all works, but the short explanation is that we spend so much time as we grow up building defenses to make sure we do not get hurt. A primary objective for most of us is avoiding pain. Believing that others can hurt you means a portion of your mind searches for ways to minimize this threat.

Imagine what happens when you get married, but you believe in your heart that you are not lovable or worthy of mature and Christ-like affection. Imagine feeling like you must pretend to be someone you are not because "no one could possibly love the *real you.*" You will tend to keep people – even your spouse – at arm's length. If you do let your defenses down and allow the deep intimacy of a healthy marriage, you may feel vulnerable and unsafe. In many situations, people create a self-fulfilling prophecy. They do not believe themselves to be loveable, so they act in ways that make it hard for their spouse to have loving actions and feelings toward them.

To make the situation even more complicated, your spouse also comes to the relationship with his or her own wounds. Two wounded people trying to find wholeness in their relationships with each other is a recipe for a troubled marriage.

Our emotional pains and hurts not only cause relationship problems, they also produce physical illness and pain. In my work as a psychologist, I specialized in treating people who had a physical disease. I studied and worked with people on the emotional aspects of chronic pain, cancer, and heart disease. Most of the patients I worked with in the chronic pain center had a childhood history of abuse or neglect. My observations are backed by science. Research into the issue shows a strong correlation between emotional trauma and physical disease.

While researchers do not completely understand this connection, I think it makes intuitive sense. Abusive or inadequate parenting creates the conditions for not only emotional pain but spiritual disconnect as well. I have heard from hundreds of people over the years whose faith was shattered because of what they experienced. "Where was God when I was being beaten?" "If God loves me, how could He let that happen to me? He must not love me."

A physical explanation also exists. Abuse is a stressful experience. Stress causes specific changes in our bodies that you will learn about in chapter six. Experiencing chronic stress over years (and even decades) takes a physical toll on the human body. God did not design our bodies to tolerate elevated levels of stress hormones (like cortisol), blood pressure, and heart rate for extended periods of time. Without periods of rest and recuperation, we keep demanding our bodies to push forward, even when our bodies lack the resources to properly function. This only gets worse as we age, especially into our 40s. Things start to break down, and pain and symptoms start to emerge.

Put these pieces together into a whole picture and you can see that emotional wounding functions to support our enemy's objectives of keeping us so distracted with troubled relationships and dysfunctional health that we have nothing left to pursue God's purpose for our lives.

We become paralyzed. With so much noise and so much to manage, we crowd out God's voice. Not only do we lack the energy to obey His direction for us, but we don't even *hear* His direction for us! How can we? If God's voice is "still, small," or a "gentle whisper" as the NIV describes (1 Kings 19:12), there is no way our spiritual ears will be able to detect His words to us if we keep the commotion and chatter going on in our minds.

Chapter Two: What Is the Solution?

Of course, you "know" in your mind that God is the solution. He is Jehovah Rapha, the Lord God our Healer, the one who restores all things new again. But you probably don't "know" how to access the healing available to all of those in Christ Jesus. This book will teach you one important step along your path of healing – the ability to become still. Once you are still, then you will know He is God. You will *know* Him as Jehovah Rapha. You will *know* Him as Elohim, Lord God Almighty. You will *know* Him – His love, His mercies, His grace, His justice, His longsuffering nature, and His will to give you the desires of your heart.

When you reach the outer limits of what psychotherapy can provide, when medications fail you over time, when eating well and exercising take but a portion of the pain away, only a supernatural encounter with God Almighty Himself can fix the problem permanently and completely.

He can make all things new again, including your heart. When your hurting heart is finally healed, you will be able to remember the offenses, the unfair circumstances, the betrayals, and the heartbreaks but without the pain or negative emotion that surrounds those memories right now. You will know you are healed when those issues no longer have control over you and your emotions – they have become nothing more than a memory and a part of the story of your testimony of the faithfulness of God.

In sessions with my clients, we work toward a moment of stillness, and then we pray to God, laying bare the specific wound for which the person wants healing. We ask God to talk intimately, directly, and specifically to the person. Within seconds, she or he usually hears His voice or sees an image He creates for them. The individualized message carries with it the gravitas of the truth of none other than the Creator of the universe, the One who spoke all things into existence.

The sheer enormity of this direct encounter with God breaks down defenses and has the immediate effect of instant healing. The pain is gone because you have been lovingly and tenderly ministered to by the One whose breath is in your lungs. You have, in a moment, been transformed into a more total person, no longer bound by the wound from your past.

It is beautiful, and it can happen for you. When you reach this place, and the healing is sure and true, you will be able to move more confidently and boldly in the purpose that God has for you. The book of Hebrews describes what happens when the burdens of the past are lifted away from you: "…..stripping off every unnecessary weight and the sin which so easily and cleverly entangles us, let us run with endurance and active persistence the race that is set before us" (12:1, AMP).

God tells us that when we no longer allow ourselves to be bound by unnecessary weight (emotional baggage, fear, tension, worry, discouragement, depression) that entangles us, then we can move forward with the endurance required for the race that God set before us. How can you run with endurance if you are entangled by unnecessary baggage?

Your healing journey is essential to living out the reason God has you here. If that is not motivation enough to keep you engaged and willing to try this new approach to hearing God and His intimate message to you, then what would be enough? It all starts with being still. Read on…..

My Personal Encounter with Jehovah Rapha

I write this book not only from the client experiences I have had over the years but also from a deeply personal encounter with God, in which He healed me of emotional hurts that I did not even know I had. He took me through a process, and then He told me, "I want you to do this for My people." That's you. Here is my story:

I have worked as an executive coach since 2002. Before my coaching career, I held a clinical faculty appointment as a psychologist at a major teaching hospital on the east coast. Around 2013, I started to feel a tug on my heart to do something different.

Up to that time, most of my business focused on offering one-on-one coaching services. I enjoyed the privilege of working with clients who are business owners, leaders, and professionals across a wide array of industries.

However, I was starting to feel restless. I also became more and more concerned about the deteriorating mental health conditions in our country. Earlier, I reviewed the devastating statistics of the current state of mental health in this country. Having been in therapeutic services since 1991, it was obvious that people are hurting now far more than ever.

The real-life results of the spreading sense of emptiness, worry, fear, and overwhelm manifests in the heroin epidemic. In the community in which I live, people are dying *every week* from drug addiction. The families are left behind with intense grief, loss, and anger at deaths that should have been avoidable. While I knew I did not want to return to working as a psychologist and offering therapy, I knew that God wanted to me somehow reach a bigger audience around this issue.

Since I knew God gave me the vision to reach larger groups of people, I developed something I refer to as the "Abrahamic syndrome." Perhaps you have some familiarity with this? God gives you a vision or a word, and you say, "OK, God, I'll take it from here." Off you go, pursuing YOUR goals and not necessarily God's goals. This is exactly what Abraham did when God told him he would have a child and that child did not arrive in the timeframe Abraham thought it would. He took matters into his own hands and had a child, Ishmael, with a handmaiden in his household. This was not the child God promised him. The promised child, Isaac, came later. But Abraham's attempts to pursue the promise in his own way set the stage for the problems in the world to this day.

I did the same thing. I assumed God wanted me to take the work I do with individual clients and turn it into a recorded, downloadable program to sell on the internet. This way I could help more people build a business and career with less stress and overwhelm.

Over the course of three years, I spent $30,000 developing and marketing this program. And it generated *not a dime*. It did not make one cent. By God's grace, I have a wonderfully supportive husband who in no way made me feel guilty or ashamed about this tremendous failure.

I was not so merciful toward myself. At a certain point in situations like this, you realize you have to "stop the bleeding." It was a very tough decision to make because I had put in so much money and time that I thought I could not just stop.

I did eventually pull the plug and torpedoed the project. While no one in my life ever made me feel ashamed, I did feel guilty. How could I not? It was compounded by the fact that I believed I was following God's will for my life and business. Why didn't this work? What was going on?

I spent several months licking my wounds. Although I did not discover the source of my problem for a while, I did eventually move through the tough emotions of such an experience. But then I was faced with a huge question: "What am I supposed to do now?"

I knew God was calling me away from what I had been doing. That was crystal clear, and I was ready to phase out of individual work. But what was I supposed to phase INTO? Through the miracle of Facebook, I had developed a close friendship with a woman who lived in California, the other side of the country from my hometown in Pennsylvania. Debra had become a spiritual mentor and a dear friend. I have learned so much from her about the depth of Jesus' work on the cross.

One day, Debra told me she was going to start a five-day period of fasting so she could hear a word from the Lord. When Debra fasts, she FASTS. She goes without food for days at a time. Up until that moment, I had never gone a day without food in my life – why would someone do something so extreme? I had fasted before, using the general principles of the Daniel Fast, but nothing more restrictive than that.

On a whim, I told Debra, "Hey, I'll fast with you!" This was clearly a Holy Spirit moment because it seemed insane. But there I was, volunteering to go for one whole day without food in solidarity with Debra. We decided to start the next day. If you have ever done a fast before, you probably know that it is best to prepare spiritually and mentally before starting. It can be an intense process, and it is important to be "prayed up" beforehand. Even though I was committing to fast with absolutely no preparation beforehand, I threw caution to the wind.

The first day, I only had a handful of cashews. I felt a bit weak but, overall, not as bad as I thought I would. I extended my fast to a second day. On the night of the third day (when I transitioned to a

Daniel fast), I started having wildly prophetic dreams. This happened on three consecutive nights, and I interpreted them as confirmation that God wanted me to continue the fast.

Over the next few days, I decided that I would fast for 21 days. I had done that before and felt comfortable. But God had other ideas – He kept putting the idea in my head of a 40-day fast. I told Him, "Lord, I DON'T WANT TO DO a 40-day fast."

He did not give up. On day 9, I relented and determined to fast for 40 days. One day each week I did not eat any food, and the remaining six days I ate only fruits and vegetables.

God rewarded me mightily with major revelations for which I was unprepared but profoundly grateful. While I thought I was fasting to hear a word from Him about my business, He told me in my quiet time, "I want My way with YOU." He wanted me to submit myself to Him and hear His input on me. I was nervous, but I obeyed.

The next morning, I sat in my prayer closet for about an hour and a half. I prayed out loud and submitted myself to Him. This was hard for me – I am a hard-charging, ambitious, goal-directed person. He was telling me, "Anita, I don't want you to 'do' anything except open your mind and heart to what I want to tell you."

I know you may have had a moment like this, one in which God wants your full attention and your total submission. Maybe you have surrendered to Him, and maybe you have not. I chose to surrender to Him. And He healed me of deep emotional wounds *that I did not even know I had!*

God has blessed me mightily throughout my life. My parents were wonderful. They loved me and my brother, and they fully supported us in our life and academic decisions. They spent time with us, and it was a lovely childhood. It wasn't perfect, of course, but I always counted myself supremely blessed because of the family horror stories I had heard from others throughout my career. In the process, I minimized – or more accurately, I totally ignored – the ways in which my parents' emotional hurts downloaded onto me.

While my parents doted on us, growing up in an ambitious family has its downsides. We never felt pressured to perform, per se, but there was a high level of tension and anxiety in the house. I knew my mother had a problem with anxiety. However, I never considered how her anxiety made me feel growing up….until God showed me.

He showed me how, as a small child, I would view my parents' anxiety and stress as a signal that we were constantly under some vague type of threat. How could I be safe if my own parents were worried and fretful about our safety?

In my unsophisticated child's mind, I translated this into a lie that I believed my entire life up until that moment in my prayer closet when God broke the chain of bondage to that lie. I believed the falsehood that "I need to control my life to make sure that I am never in danger or vulnerable."

The seductive part of lies from the enemy is that they seem to have positive results. The Type-A mentality I developed helped me drive forward and achieve big goals. I obtained my PhD in clinical psychology and then earned my license to legally practice as a psychologist. Along the way, I got married and had two beautiful boys whom I had the privilege of homeschooling.

But my hard-charging nature caught up with me. When I tackled the project that consumed $30,000, I was at the end of myself. *I had never started something I did not successfully finish.* My coping strategy of "trying harder" and pushing myself failed me.

This is the point at which God met me, when I felt broken and lost. Before He could heal me of the bondage I was in – bondage to the lie that I controlled my life and was responsible for what happened – *I had to allow Him access to my mind.* Keeping my brain busy all the time kept Him OUT.

Here are the specific steps I needed to take before healing could take place:

1. I had to recognize that God was trying to communicate with me.
2. I had to accept that He wanted to talk to me about what HE wanted to discuss, not what I wanted.
3. I had to allow Him to speak to me by creating the time and space, physically and mentally.
4. I had to submit to His voice and not my own. I had to BE STILL.
5. I had to receive His message, although it meant I had to momentarily experience the emotional hurt of acknowledging how vulnerable and unsafe I felt.

Once God spoke directly to my wounded heart, healing was immediate. I cried the same tears that Anna cried – not of sadness, but of relief and release. The struggle was over, period. And I had not even, until that moment, particularly felt like I had been struggling.

He told me that He is in control (and I am not), that I am to let HIM do "the heavy lifting" (yes, God speaks to me like that!), and that He does have a plan for me for when I stop trying to do "my" plan. Over the rest of the fasting period, God continued to push me to excavate my heart, to break down the defensive walls I had built up over the decades and allow Him to speak healing truth to me. He spoke directly, intimately, and lovingly.

But I had to submit to His will.

I had BE STILL in spirit, mind, and body.

I had to identify the core lies I believed about myself (that I was useless, I was worthless and with nothing to contribute, and I must control my life or God will stop blessing us).

I had to apologize and repent about believing – and then acting on – these lies.

Then I had to have a quiet, stilled, settled, and surrendered mind before I could hear God's voice speak directly to those painful wounds. And when He spoke, His words were a soothing balm flowing over my heart, immediately healing those hurts in my heart. He will do that for you too. In fact, it is time to do *something*, and to do it fast, because of the lethality of our crisis of emotional and spiritual decay.

Anna's experience is all too common. Regardless of what drives the increased rates of depression and anxiety, standard treatment is failing. While symptoms may decrease after medications or counseling, they manage to come back after a period of time. Medical and psychological care – even Christ-centered care – cannot heal, cure, or in any way imply that a problem is permanently gone. This is how western medicine functions. When the goal is only symptom relief and not permanent healing, how can we expect people to overcome, break their chains, and THRIVE?

Of course, God is the ultimate Healer. Much of Jesus's ministry involved healing people of lifelong battles. We can claim that healing right now, through Christ, because it is available to us. As a Christian, you probably know that. But maybe you cannot figure out exactly how to claim it. You pray, perhaps you even fast, you seek spiritual counsel, you have people pray for you, yet you still hurt. Why isn't Jesus healing you? Why are you still dealing with your emotional baggage?

In the next section, I will explain how God revealed a powerful process in which He uses my education and training as a psychologist and joins it with the power of Jesus's work on the cross to allow God to heal people with emotional wounds. I call it "Holy Spirit therapy."

As with Anna, some wounds are so profound that no amount of talk therapy, and certainly not medication, can convince a person that the beliefs they developed about themselves are untrue. They feel true and seem true because a person had a personal life experience that convinced them that some part of God's Word is untrue.

Hearing a direct message from God is certainly not a new concept. There are scores of books, workshops, podcasts, and conferences dedicated to the topic of "hearing from God." Learning to discern God's voice is crucial for healing. When you seek a word from God, you need to know how to determine whether the message you get is from Him or from some other source. Studying the Bible to understand the character and promises of God forms the basis of this type of therapy.

But what I realized in working with people over the years is that there are barriers to hearing from God, and therefore barriers to healing. Some of these barriers are spiritual, and you will learn about them in chapter ten. Usually, people who regularly hear from God about the direction of their lives do not hear from Him about healing. It is a deeper level of intimacy through Jesus Christ to allow God to heal our wounded hearts. This "Holy Spirit therapy" dives deeper than simply hearing from God.

However, other barriers are purely psychological. They are things we do ourselves in our minds that keep God at arm's length. As desperately as we want Him to heal us, often we are scared of allowing Him to do so. For some readers, that will resonate. For others, it will sound kind of crazy. Who in their right mind would block healing, especially from God?

As convoluted as it sounds, we do sometimes keep our defenses tight. After all, we have spent a lifetime building them up to protect ourselves. It can feel threatening to let them down, even with the promise of hearing God's opinion on the matter. So we keep Him away from our hearts. After all, if something caused you not to trust that God will protect you, then it makes sense that you will not trust Him enough to let down your defenses.

What I have learned about Holy Spirit therapy, about allowing God to speak directly to your wounded heart to correct the lies you believe and achieve healing, is not revolutionary. But clearly something was missing – otherwise, everyone would easily access the healing available by the blood of Christ. What caused this disconnect? Why was there a gap in what we "know" (that God can and does heal) and what we actually experience (continued pain and dysfunction)?

In working with so many people in various capacities over the years, I noticed a clear reason for our inability to live out the healing that God has for us. We cannot hear the healing voice of God because we have lost the ability to quiet our minds. In fact, I would wager that you struggle with quieting your mind and turning down the volume on all the mental chatter going on inside your head.

There are so many reasons why quieting our minds and stilling ourselves does not happen easily. Our minds are simply too full to hear from God. But learning how to turn the volume down on our mental chatter ends up being a skill we have to learn before prayer can develop into the two-way conversation that God intends for His people.

As I realized the intense need for a full-blown discussion about this little-discussed aspect of hearing from God, I knew I needed to write a book about it. And I knew all along the title of the book would be, **Be Still**. I didn't know the subtitle of the book, but this verse from Psalms was the very first verse I ever intentionally decided to commit to memory. And wait until you read in chapter five about a HUGE "God-moment" around one of His many Hebrew "compound names," Jehovah-Rapha, the Lord God our Healer. Remember that Hebrew word, *rapha* because it holds the key to your healing.

Let's get started by first understanding, without a shadow of a doubt, that God wants us to be healed and whole, and He made a way for it to happen.

Chapter Three: God Has a Plan for Your Life

I hope you are beginning to understand that your healing is vitally important. It is not something that would be "nice to do" if you have time. No. Your healing will not only have a direct, positive impact on your relationships, it will also free your energy to pursue God's purpose for your life.

Some of you will not know what God's purpose for your life is. Some of you may not even fully believe that God has a purpose for your life. I promise you that He does, and I want to prove that to you by listing specific Bible verses that confirm this truth. The first step toward understanding something deeply is to know it intellectually in your mind. You may not believe these verses yet, but it is crucial to start with the foundational truths before you can eventually move them into your belief system.

Consider for a moment why Jesus Christ would start His public ministry declaring that He was sent to heal the brokenhearted. Nothing in the Bible is insignificant or coincidental. God knows that as long as the state of your heart remains broken, you will not move forward in the purpose He has for you. And He does have a purpose for you! Let us dive into Scripture to find this truth. I love Hebrews 13:20-21 because it so clearly points out that God does have a purpose for individual people, not "just" for the nation of Israel:

> Now may the God of peace who brought again
> from the dead our Lord Jesus, the great shepherd
> of the sheep, by the blood of the eternal

> covenant, equip you with everything good that
> you may do His will, working in us that which is
> pleasing in His sight, through Jesus Christ, to
> whom be the glory forever and ever. Amen.

I mentioned the nation of Israel because perhaps the most well-known verse about God's purpose is Jeremiah 29:11. In this passage, God is speaking through Jeremiah to the whole nation, not to one person specifically. However, 2 Timothy 3:16-17 tells us that "All Scripture is given to us by inspiration of God, and is profitable for doctrine, for reproof, for correction, for instruction in righteousness, that the man of God may be complete, thoroughly equipped for every good work." Therefore, we can rightly assume that God can speak to us about His truth through all Scripture when properly applied. Let us then claim Jeremiah's statement as true for each of us: "For I know the thoughts that I think toward you, says the LORD, thoughts of peace and not of evil, to give you a future and hope."

In 1 Corinthians chapter 12, Paul speaks at length about how God knows exactly what He is doing with the various gifts, talents, and skills He has bestowed upon us. We learn in this chapter that God puts us together in the body of Christ like pieces of a puzzle, or members of a physical body, so that each person contributes according to his or her ability. When each person does that, the whole body can properly function. How could this be true if God did not have an individual and unique purpose for each person?

"But now God has set the members, each one of them, in the body just as He pleased. And if they were all one member, where would the body be?" (1 Cor 12:18-19). Paul continues his exhortation that God has a grand plan for us in Philippians 1:6. I believe this verse hints at the idea that if we, during our time in the natural world, do not fully achieve what He planned for us, He will make it complete when Christ comes again. This relieves me of any pressure of "having to get it right." God knows our struggles and why we hold back: "And I am sure of this, that He who began a good work in you will bring it to completion at the day of Jesus Christ."

In Proverbs 3:5-6, we learn that when we submit our hearts to God and lean on Him, He will make our paths straight. That means we *have* a path, implying that the path goes somewhere and has an objective. That path will likely be crooked until we trust Him with the direction – then He will make that path straight so we can travel down it more easily. "Trust in the LORD with all your heart and lean not on your own understanding; in all your ways submit to Him and He will make your paths straight."

Returning to Hebrews, we see that God will reward us according to what He has promised us. Under what circumstances does He reward us? When we do His will! So doing His will is what He has planned for us. He has a plan for YOU! And that plan is to do His will. We need to understand His will for us so we can then operate inside it. "You need to persevere so that when you have done the will of God, you will receive what He has promised" (Heb 10:36).

I absolutely love this next verse because it spells out the overall goal God has for us. He wants us to use what He has given us for the good of other people! He did not give you gifts, talents, and skills for yourself alone but to help care for other people in His name. Why would each of us have strengths and gifts if not to use for His purposes in His kingdom? "As each one has received a gift, minister it to one another, as good stewards of the manifold grace of God" (1 Pet 4:10).

The writer of Psalms tells us that by yielding to God, He will bring "our way" to pass. You have a "way," things you desire in your heart, that He put there for His reasons. We never have to follow His directions for our lives – it is completely within our free will to be openly rebellious. However, submitting ourselves to His will means He brings the outcome to fruition, and we can reap the rewards. Doesn't that sound attractive? "Delight yourself also in the LORD, and He shall give you the desires of your heart. Commit your way to the LORD, trust also in Him, and He shall bring it to pass" (Ps 37:4-5).

The entire book of Acts points to the idea that God has a purpose for all of us, no matter our station in life. But this specific passage shows that God directs us. Why would He do that if He did not have His purpose to achieve through us? "Now after he [Paul] had seen the vision, immediately we sought to go to Macedonia, concluding that the Lord had called us to preach the gospel to them" (Acts 16:10).

I pray these verses speak to you, helping you grow in the truth that God has a purpose for your life, and that remaining overwhelmed by emotional "stuff" only holds us back from achieving what God wants to do through us.

The next step – understanding that God wants to heal you!

Chapter Four: God's Objective to Healing Your Wounds!

God has a plan for your life. You may know this, especially after reading the previous chapter, but still feel discouraged, defeated, or even fearful of pursuing that plan. Maybe all the hurts, struggles, and "junk" you deal with on a daily basis take so much of your time and energy that you cannot even focus on doing what God wants you to do. Isn't that a major tactic of the enemy, to keep us busy and overwhelmed and distracted so that we do not have time or motivation to move forward on His agenda?

But I want to assure you – actually, I want to promise you – that God wants to heal you! I know it is very important to Him because so many places in His Word He directly or indirectly states His desire to heal and bring wholeness. Please read on for just a small portion of the Scriptures that speak to healing.

But before diving into Scripture, I want to put up some cautions in our expectations of what God will do for us, and others. This starts with a very basic premise: In the Bible, God means what HE means to say, not what "we think" He means to say. This sounds obvious, but sometimes we set ourselves up for disappointment in assuming that a particular outcome "should" happen. If it doesn't, it means either that we didn't have enough faith or that God doesn't love us, or even something worse like God must not be true.

God promises healing. There is no doubt about this, and you will read the verses that prove it. However, He means the healing He wills for you, not necessarily the healing outcome you want. Yes, Jesus Christ took our sickness and sins on the cross, and we can claim victory over those mental and physical issues. However, sometimes that victory is not won in the natural. Sometimes we are not healed (partially or fully) in our earthly lifetime. Sometimes we do not access the healing God has for us until we go to be with Him for eternity.

When I think about this reality of infirmities (that we can claim God's healing, but it must be on His terms, not ours), I recall the events in the book of Daniel with Shadrach, Meshach, and Abed-Nego. When King Nebuchadnezzar threatened to throw them in the fiery furnace, their response is exactly the one we need to have when faced with challenging situations:

> Shadrach, Meshach, and Abed-Nego answered and said to the king, "O, Nebuchadnezzar, we have no need to answer you in this matter. If that is the case, our God whom we serve is able to deliver us from the burning fiery furnace, and He will deliver us from your hand, O king. But if not, let it be known to you, O king, that we do not serve your gods, nor will we worship the gold image which you have set up." (Dan 3:16-18)

What these men conveyed is a good model for how to manage our own expectations of deliverance out of struggles. They declared that the Lord God is able to deliver them, but if deliverance is not His will in the natural realm, then they will still be saved. They will not go against the God of Abraham, Isaac, and Jacob but will instead die. They trusted that God would save them, even if the fire killed them. Of course, their outcome is nothing short of breathtaking. As the king watched them in the furnace, he saw *four men* walking around, when only three were thrown in. And that fourth man "is like the Son of God" (Dan 3:25). The preincarnate Jesus Christ was protecting and delivering them from the fire.

When you pursue healing, please know that God WILL heal you, but according to His wishes. Realistically, most people, when they learn to still their minds and really hear God's voice, get immediate emotional healing in an area of their lives. This almost always happens. It is also true that God does not TOTALLY heal us of every wound we have. That simply is not how things work. If it did, we could be perfect – and that is not possible.

Consider that Paul had some significant challenge that he prayed for God to make "depart" from him, but God did not give him his requested relief.

> And lest I should be exalted above measure by the abundance of the revelations, a thorn in the flesh was given to me, a messenger of Satan to buffet me, lest I be exalted above measure. Concerning this thing I pleaded with the Lord three times that it might depart from me. And He said to me, "My grace is sufficient for you, for My strength is made perfect in weakness." Therefore most gladly I will rather boast in my infirmities, that the power of Christ may rest upon me. Therefore I take pleasure in my infirmities, in reproaches, in needs, in persecutions, in distresses, for Christ's sake. For when I am weak, then I am strong." (2 Cor 12:7-10)

Whether Paul's thorn was of a physical, emotional, or persecutory origin, the Lord God answered Paul's pleadings the way God wanted it to resolve, not the way Paul wanted it to resolve. Paul desperately wished to have this substantial trial removed from his worldly experience, but God had a different idea. I wish I had a more satisfying explanation for why these things happen, but I do not.

I fall back on the truth that God's thoughts and ways are higher than our ways (Isa 55:8-9) and that God works in all things for the good of those who have been called to His purpose (Rom 8:28). When we go through our own trials, we try to remember that God is sovereign, and His grace and mercy are with us. We are never promised that He will always swoop in and save us according to our wishes. In many instances, He does, and He said we should come to Him and ask in faith (Mt 21:22; 1 Jn 5:14; Jn 14:13), knowing we will receive what we ask for. What we receive, even if it is in accordance with His will, happens on His timeline and in His way, always.

I go to lengths to say this because sometimes God wants to speak to us about one thing and heal one area, but we want another area healed. Guess what? What we are focused on doesn't end up happening. It can feel discouraging and lead us down a very tough spiritual path. Please know that you will be ultimately healed in eternity, even if you only get a small glimpse of that healing here in the natural realm. This can feel challenging to accept, but it is crucial that you understand how God sees things. He is concerned about eternity, as well as the here and now. He knows your future into infinity. We are assured healing of everything at some point. Have faith.

Let us return to examining some of God's promises of healing in His Word. I like to start with Jesus's own words as he began His public ministry as recorded in the book of Luke. He stood up in the synagogue and read the words from the prophet Isaiah concerning the coming Messiah. Pay close attention to the reason He gives for being "sent" here:

> And when He had opened the book, He found the place where it was written:
>
> "The Spirit of the LORD is upon Me, Because He has anointed Me To preach the gospel to the poor;
>
> He has sent me to *heal the brokenhearted*, (emphasis added) To proclaim liberty to the captives And recovery of sight to the blind,
>
> To set at liberty those who are oppressed; To proclaim the acceptable year of the LORD.'" (4:17b-19, NKJV)

Jesus Christ came to heal your broken heart. Think about that for just a moment – resist the urge to move on from this monumental truth. His stated purpose, after His time in the wilderness and being tempted by Satan, is to heal your heart that has been bruised and battered, broken and shattered. God knows the hurts you have sustained, the struggles you endure, the challenges you face, and the pain and heartache you carry. He is not oblivious. Of all the things Christ could have publicly stated at the start of His earthly ministry, he chose to address our broken-heartedness instead of physical infirmities. That is how much He is aware of what we go through on a daily basis. He recognizes exactly how much emotional pain causes more problems than even physical pain. Our woundedness is so profound that Christ wanted us to know first thing, after the gospel, that He has arrived for the specific purpose of emotional healing. He provided a path.

I could write an entire book on just these verses and how they relate to healing and wholeness by themselves. The use of the words "captive" and "oppressed" speak even more deeply to the weightiness of His powerful ministry. For example, he proclaims liberty for the captives. A captive is someone who has been captured and held against their will. They are not prisoners in the sense that captives are not those who commit a crime and become prisoners because of lawlessness. No, a captive is a victim, the target of someone who illegitimately is holding her against her will. The same situation happens with those who are "oppressed." The oppressed are held down and subjugated immorally or illegally.

The things that happened to you that were unfair, unjust, immoral, and evil have held you captive for years, or perhaps even decades. You have been oppressed with feelings of unworthiness, dirtiness, unlovability, lack of confidence, discouragement, and defeat. These spirits that have oppressed you must yield and flee in the name of Jesus Christ (Mt 8:32; Jas 4:7) because He came to set you free from all things that oppress and take you captive illegitimately. The situations themselves may not change, and we certainly cannot alter what has happened in the past. But the impact of those events that created spirits of rejection, emotional struggle, troubled relationships, emptiness, and overwhelm have been defeated by the power of Jesus Christ and His authority that we can appropriate in His name!

While this passage in Luke carries sufficient weight to prove the fact that God wants to heal you, we can see more evidence of it throughout all of Scripture. We start with the passage from Isaiah that Jesus Christ quoted:

> The Spirit of the LORD GOD is upon Me,
> Because the LORD has anointed Me To preach

good tidings to the poor, He has sent Me to heal the brokenhearted, To proclaim liberty to the captives, And the opening of the prison to those who are bound. (Isa 61:1)

Surely He has borne our griefs And carried our sorrow; Yet we esteemed Him stricken, Smitten by God, and afflicted, But he was wounded for our transgressions, He was bruised for our iniquities; the chastisement for our peace was upon Him, And by His stripes we are healed. (Isa 53:4-5)

The LORD is near to those who have a broken heart, And saves such as have a contrite spirit. (Ps 24:18)

He heals the brokenhearted and binds up their wounds. (Ps 147:3)

For I am the LORD who heals you. (Exo 15:26b)

My wayward children, says the LORD, come back to me, and I will heal your wayward hearts. (Jer 3:22, NLT)

Heal me, O LORD, and I shall be healed; save me, and I shall be saved: for You are my praise. (Jer 17:14)

He himself bore our sins in His body on the tree, that we might die to sin and live to righteousness. By His wounds you have been healed. (1 Pet 2:24)

Confess your trespasses to one another, and pray for one another, that you may be healed. The effective, fervent prayer of a righteous man avails much. (Jas 5:16)

And when He had called His twelve disciples over to Him, He gave them power over unclean spirits, to cast them out, and to heal all kinds of disease. (Matt 10:1)

But when Jesus knew it, He withdrew from there. And great multitudes followed Him, and He healed them all. (Matt 12:15)

And when Jesus went out He saw a great multitude; and He was moved with compassion for them, and healed their sick. (Matt 14:14)

And when the men of that place recognized Him, they sent out into all that surrounding region, brought to Him all who were sick, and begged Him that they might only touch the hem of His garment. And as many as touched it were made perfectly well. (Matt 14:35-36)

And he said to her, "Daughter, your faith has made you well. Go in peace, and be healed of your affliction." (Mark 5:34)

By stretching out Your hand to heal, and that signs and wonders may be done through the name of Your holy Servant, Jesus. (Acts 4:30)

If any part of your mind still doubts God's sincere and true desire to heal you, I urge you to do a Bible study on this topic. I only included a portion of the Scriptural references to healing, so please dive in more deeply to this very important topic.

And remember Hebrews 12:1 describes what happens when we set aside "every weight" and the "sin which so easily ensnares us." When our emotional pains are healed, they will no longer be a burden on our shoulders, weighing us down with discouragement, rejection, depression, overwhelm, stress, and anxiety. These things "ensnare" us, they hold us back. When we are free, we can then "run with endurance the race that is set before us."

God has a "race" set before you, a path, purpose, and future for you to pursue with endurance. The trials of life, and the actions of the enemy, cause us to stumble and slow down in that pursuit. Your personal healing will unleash and redirect the energy you currently have to expend simply getting through the day managing your emotional struggles. Imagine when those struggles are gone –

consider for one moment how freedom will allow you to more boldly and confidently show up in God's kingdom. Your world will expand and grow, bringing others along with you in your expansion.

Your healed heart will release you to do the things that feel too intimidating and overwhelming right now. When you stop living every day from a defensive stance and stop living out of your wounded and broken heart, suddenly the world opens up in a different way. Not only can you feel better, but your relationships can improve. You will not be "perfect," of course, as none of us can be. We are "made" perfect by the blood of Jesus Christ for eternity. In the meantime, we must constantly be open to the areas God wants to heal and make whole as we are conformed more closely to the image of Christ (Rom 8:29). Each step in that conformation process means we are more Christ-like in our world. That spreads the gospel and helps us serve God's kingdom by filling the needs of His people. We can do that more effectively when we are not limited by our own hurts and pains.

Biblical Examples of Healed Hearts

While God speaks quite a bit about His attention to the state of our heart and our emotional lives, the New Testament examples of healing involve either spiritual or physical healing. Certainly, the relationship between our emotional, spiritual, and physical parts overlaps extensively, and each one impacts the other two in dramatic and direct ways. I mentioned earlier that my professional training immersed me in the scientific understanding of the mind-body connection. Research has shown for decades that our emotional life influences our physical state, and vice versa. You will also read later in this book how our spiritual condition (specifically our readiness to forgive) impacts our physical and emotional health to such a degree that secular researchers study this connection. Therefore, we can safely assume that God, in healing physically and spiritually, also causes emotional growth.

We find an example in John 9:1-41. Jesus miraculously gives sight to a man blind from birth. After Jesus gives him sight, the man speaks with courage and conviction to the religious leaders who intend to kill Jesus. Read how this man defended Jesus:

> The man answered and said to them, "Why, this
> is a marvelous thing, that you do not know

where He is from; yet He has opened my eyes! Now we know that God does not hear sinners; but if anyone is a worshiper of God and does His will, He hears him. Since the world began it has been unheard of that anyone opened the eyes of one how was born blind. If this Man were not from God, He would do nothing." (30-33)

What bravery! While we know nothing about this man's personality before this event, his outspokenness afterward causes him to be cast out by the powerful religious leaders. Would we have the courage to speak out for the truth of Jesus Christ at the risk of being cast out and socially rejected? Physical healing and restoration at this magnitude gave this man – and the others whom Jesus healed – the emotional capacity to proclaim the truth.

Let us turn now to some Old Testament prophets, who are entirely human and relatable. Many of them have false beliefs about who they are, what they can do, and how God can use them until God Himself speaks directly to that wrong belief.

In Jeremiah, we see the young prophet reacting to God as you and I certainly would if we received a similar word from the Lord:

> Then the word of the Lord came to [Jeremiah], saying, "Before I formed you in the womb I knew you; Before you were born I sanctified you; I ordained you a prophet to the nations." Then [Jeremiah] said, "Ah, Lord God! Behold, I cannot speak, for I am a youth." (1:4-6)

When confronted with a great challenge, Jeremiah's defense mechanisms kicked in. He immediately deployed the deep belief he had about himself and attempted to use it as an excuse for not obeying God's command. He tells God that he is too young. He believed he did not have the training, experience, and wisdom required for the job God gave him. This is identical to what happens to each of us: we have a challenge before us, or some event presents itself, that triggers our doubts, worries, sense of incompetence, and belief of being good enough. We then behave according to those lies. We withhold, we withdraw, we retreat, we make excuses. In short, we act as if these lies were true.

But let us examine what happens in this instance. Jeremiah tells God what he believes about himself at his core. He believes he lacks the competence to meet these demands. Jeremiah does what we all need to do in order to have God correct our lies with His unchanging truth – he bares his wrong belief to God directly.

How does God react? In the way that He always reacts when we come to Him baring our wounded hearts and souls. He gives Jeremiah a word that instantly corrects his wrong self-concept. Jeremiah's identity is immediately brought out of the world of lies and into alignment with the one true God who formed him in his mother's womb. How does God do this? With a direct, intimate word:

> But the Lord said to me: "Do not say, *I am a youth*, For you shall go to all to whom I send you, And whatever I command you, you shall speak. Do not be afraid of their faces, For I am with you to deliver you," says the Lord. Then the Lord put forth His hand and touched my mouth, and the Lord said to me, "Behold, I have put My words in your mouth." (1:7-9)

With this sentence, Jeremiah is healed of his wrong beliefs. We no longer hear of his doubts and inadequacies, and he learns the truth about who he is, and who God is. In an instant, Jeremiah's emotional blockage comes down, and he opens his heart to God's work through him. We see this impact on Jeremiah right away, as he has the courage to report to God the visions the Lord gave him of an almond branch and a pot of boiling water. Jeremiah realized the truth, that God will give him what he needs and that his insecurities were obstacles to God's work.

Emotional healing matters. We see this also in the story of Moses. Like Jeremiah, when God calls Moses to leadership, Moses' reaction is one of incompetence and unworthiness: "But Moses said to God, 'Who am I that I should go to Pharaoh, and that I should bring the children of Israel out of Egypt?'" (Exod 3:11)

Does this comment seem familiar to you? Have you ever thought the same thing, or maybe even stated it out loud? Have you ever believed that the task you were called to, either by God or by a boss at work, exceeded your capability? Maybe you have thought, "I'm unqualified, not educated, have no credentials, and don't like to speak in front of groups." While it may be true you don't like to speak in front of groups, the reason you don't is probably based on one of the lies mentioned before. Look at how God responds to Moses: "I will certainly be with you. And this shall be a sign to you that I have sent you: When you have brought the people out of Egypt, you shall serve God on this mountain" (Exod 3:12).

God does not address Moses' insecurities directly. Instead, He tells Moses something far more powerful and useful: that God Himself will accompany him. Then He follows up with giving Moses a glimpse into the future. This is how God the Father takes care of His children. He tells us what we really need to know, which overrides our irrational excuses and then sets us on a powerful path to set His people free.

Of course, Moses did not stop with this one point of insecurity. He was worried that people would not believe him and then finally tried to convince God that He was wrong because his speech impediment disqualified him. What did God do? He reminded Moses of who He is:

> So the LORD said to him, "Who has made man's mouth? Or who makes the mute, the deaf, the seeing, or the blind? Have not I, the LORD? Now therefore, go, and I will be with your mouth and teach you what you shall say." (Exod 4:11-12)

God speaks to our deepest fears and anxieties and tells us what we need to know. This direct and personal word from Him sets us on the proper path. In Moses' case, he still had residual doubts, so God worked around them by providing a solution. Notice that God did not give up on Moses, nor did He chastise him. After all of this, Moses embarks on his God-ordained mission to free the Israelites from Egypt.

God heals our emotional baggage. He has always done it throughout history, and since God never changes, He continues to do it today.

Chapter Five: What Is Stillness?

Missy A. had attended one of my Be Still conferences. She is a woman after God's heart, dedicated to learning about God. Her dream is to study apologetics and spread the gospel; however, she kept God at arm's length. Despite accepting Jesus Christ as her savior, she resisted giving Him access to her heart. Essentially, Missy did not trust God.

After just the first night of the conference, Missy started experiencing God in a different way, and she decided to drop her defenses just a little. That is all God needs to speak in a powerful and life-altering way. She sent me a message describing what happened to her:

> Everything you said in your introduction, I had heard before, but this time it was like I "really" heard it. When you went over the list of why we avoid hearing from God, I thought, *OK, I know this is true; this is why I don't hear from Him. What happens when I relax?* And loud and clear, God instantly revealed a lie that I believe. It is sad to admit, but the lie was, "God hates me and wants to punish me." I walked away that night knowing the lie and trusting that God would walk with me in this healing.
>
> Two days later, I felt so burdened and I prayed. He revealed to me that I was worrying about my daughter, and that I need to trust in Him. The burden immediately lifted. Then the next day, I heard God speak to me what I needed to hear! It

was soft and matter of fact. I was driving in my car, not really thinking about anything.

He said to me, "You're going to heaven and there is nothing you need to do." Immediately, I realized that I had a list in my head of the wrongs I needed to right to be in God's love, and He simply said, "There is no list."

I felt this peace in my heart! I am still adjusting to this feeling of being where I am instead of wanting to be at this destination in my mind (and always feeling condemned for not being there). All I can say is WOW, praise God; thank you Jesus and the power of the Holy Spirit!

As you learn about biblical stillness, you will find how much it involves letting go of control, and a deliberate invitation to allow God into your heart. You will learn later in the book about the barriers we put up that delay or prevent our healing. Missy had one of those barriers, but she decided to pull down that block and let her mind be still, and God spoke to her. The key is understanding stillness – what it is biblically and how we can put ourselves in that position.

I invite you to take just three minutes to reflect on the following questions before you continue reading: What is stillness? How will you know when you are being still? What will be different?

If you did not take those three minutes to reflect on answering these questions, I suggest thinking about why you did not do it. Knowing human nature, approximately 93% of readers did not take those three minutes. If you kept on reading, you are not alone!

I think the resistance to taking time to explore important ideas helps explain why most people avoid stillness. The truth is that achieving stillness in mind and body requires time and space. In our modern lifestyle, we don't like things that take time. We like to save time or multitask so we extract more out of time. Stillness requires – at a bare minimum – slowing down. In a fast-paced world, slowing down just doesn't cut it. Who has time to slow down?

Let us return to Psalm 46:10. God tells us, "Be still, and know that I am God." That sounds like a directive to me. It is not an option.

Let us also examine the order of the directive – He tells us FIRST to be still, and then we can know that He is God. Think about how different this verse would be if the order were reversed: Know that I am God and be still.

God wants something from us. He wants us to do the things that are best for us and for His kingdom. If He wanted to, He could pull a heavy-handed power play, bypassing our free will and forcing us to acknowledge Him as God. Then we would be coerced into submission.

But God gave us free will. He allows us to choose to draw near to Him and to know Him. Therefore, He tells us the order in which things happen best in His kingdom – first, we become still and then we are positioned to more fully and completely know that He is God. He doesn't want to storm into your life, demanding, "I am God, so be still." That places God in a more intimidating, almost aggressive attitude, something that is most assuredly contrary to His nature.

When we get in proper alignment with Him, the position of stillness, we will automatically "know" He is God. Again, returning to the verse, notice the use of the conjunction "and." God does not say, "Be still, then know that I am God." He uses the word "and," which grammatically is used to indicate when things happen at the same time. Think about phrases we use that imply two or more situations happening simultaneously: peanut butter and jelly, milk and cookies, bread and butter, wait and see, pencil and eraser. These objects occur together in time. This is the conjunction God uses. When we are still, we will also *at the same time* know He is God. Imagine the power in this position!

But God revealed even more to me about being still during another fast I did about a year before I wrote this book. I mentioned earlier that God made it known to me several years ago that He wanted me to write a book entitled, *Be Still.*

As I started to sketch out the content of this book, I decided to do a word study on Psalm 46:10. After all, it is the foundation of this book, so I thought it would help me to have a deeper understanding of this verse by studying the Hebrew version. This might sound academic and irrelevant, but personally, I learn so much more about God by diving into the original language in which His Word was written. And considering what God unveiled during this word study, I know I will absolutely do more of this for the rest of my life!

Let me lay the groundwork for this important revelation. In various places in the Old Testament, God's Hebrew name, Jehovah, is attached to another word. This is known as a "compound name." For instance, in Genesis 22:14, Abraham has just been prevented from completing God's instruction to sacrifice his only son, Isaac. At the very last moment, the Angel of the Lord appeared and told Abraham not to sacrifice his son. Abraham looks to the thicket and sees a ram that he then uses for the sacrifice. In recognition of how God saved Abraham's son and provided for a substitute sacrifice supernaturally, Abraham called that area, "Jehovah-Jireh," meaning "The Lord will provide." Just as God provided a sacrifice to save Isaac, this series of events and the name Abraham calls the area foreshadows God's offering of His own son as a sacrifice for all mankind.

Likewise, we see another compound name for God in Exodus 15:26. Here, Moses is leading the Israelites across the desert out of Egypt and into the promised land. At one point, they experienced a three-day period in which they had no water. When they finally came upon a source of water, it tasted bitter. Moses prayed to God for guidance, and in obedience, Moses follows God's command to throw a piece of wood into the water. The water supernaturally became drinkable (Exod 15:22-25).

God then speaks to the nation of Israel, saying, "If you diligently heed the voice of the LORD your God and do what is right in His sight, give ear to His commandments and keep all His statutes, I will put none of the diseases on you which I have brought on the Egyptians. For I am the LORD who heals you."

In Hebrew, "I am the LORD who heals you" is translated as Jehovah-Rapha. This means "the Lord our Healer" or "the LORD who heals." The God we serve, the God of Abraham, Isaac, and Jacob, is also known as our ultimate healer. It is His name and it is therefore in His nature to heal. This word, *rapha* clearly demonstrates this.

Pay attention to the word: *RAPHA*. (In Strong's Concordance, it is listed as "rapa.")

Returning to my word study of the verse Psalm 46:10, "Be still, and know that I am GOD," I sat one morning with my concordance reference books and an internet search as a back-up. As I paged through the concordance, I found the word "still" and looked at the Hebrew word associated with it from Psalm 46:10. Imagine my surprise and shock when I saw the following Hebrew word for "be still:" *RAPHAH*.

Do you see what I saw immediately? The incredible similarities between the Hebrew word for "healer" and the word for "be still?" They clearly come from the same root word! In fact, do you see that "the healer" is inside of "being still?" Do you get this significance? God is telling us that He functions as our healer when we can be still. He is inside and within being still! We can find the healer (*rapha*) inside being still (*raphah*).

Healer = *rapha*

Be still = *raphah*

My mind almost went totally blank in the shock of this revelation. Here, for years, God was telling me to write a book called, Be Still. And He wanted me to write about how He heals. He arranged His Word to be so consistent that when we follow His command to be still, we can then know He is God....and we can claim His healing.

I really hope you can receive how powerful this concept is and see the lengths God has gone to convey that His healing happens when we are still. Stillness and healing are so closely related that they are essentially the same Hebrew word.

Does this demonstrate how the healing you yearn for and seek each day starts with being still? This confirms how powerfully God communicates through His Word and that, when we draw nearer to Him, He draws nearer to us (Jas 4:8). He reveals deeper levels of who He is as we delve deeper into His Word. I praise Him every day for His use of language to convey truths that are textured and nuanced, yet relevant and timeless. How blessed we are to serve Him!

Now you see how God, through His directive to be still, has positioned us to receive His healing by knowing He is God. This then begs the question: What does it mean to be still? What happens inside stillness that postures us to receive His healing? I will answer these questions from two different perspectives: the spiritual and the psychological.

The Spirituality of Stillness

Let's dive into stillness by focusing on the Hebrew word for "be still," the word, *raphah*. According to various concordances, *raphah* connotes a range of meanings. First is the idea of "to stop striving." This is perhaps the most important psychological aspect of stillness, as well. When we cease striving, we stand down and allow other things, or God, to take control and steer the course of events. It is a posture of physical and mental stillness, of not trying to problem-solve or make something happen or worry about an event or situation. When we relax our mental and physical efforts, we stop trying. Obviously, there are times in life in which actions to create something or make something happen are acceptable and required. But when we seek healing or a word from the Lord, or when we struggle and need reassurance that He will never leave us or forsake us because of who He is, we must dial back our efforts and put an end to forcing things to happen.

In other places in the Bible, God tells us through the prophets and others about variations on stillness that help clarify what this looks like. For instance, in Exodus, Moses said to the Israelites: "Do not fear! *Stand still* and see the salvation of the LORD, which He will accomplish for you today. For the Egyptians whom you see today, you shall see again no more forever. The LORD will fight for you, and *you shall hold your peace*" (14:13,14, emphasis added).

In this passage, God gives clear instruction to His people that they are to "stand still" and to "hold your peace." In other words, He is telling them to not fight, not try, not strive to move forward, do not act out of fear and desperation. God says that when the people – YOU – stand still and hold their peace, the Lord fights for them….and for you. He does all the work. But this situation can only happen when we actively decide to stop trying to make it happen ourselves. We do this by standing still.

God has a solution for all the problems in our lives. He knows what we need, when we need it, and how to deliver it to us. But if we spend our time fretting about the situations, worrying, talking to others incessantly, and trying new and different (or even the same) coping strategies, we crowd out God. Not only are we unable to hear Him, but we create so much activity and motion that it is impossible for God to act. We dominate the situation rather than standing back, being still, and letting God dominate.

Imagine if you were sick and you went to the doctor to get help. While in the examination room, rather than letting the doctor talk and ask questions, you start talking about all the things you think could be wrong, what you have tried to do in the past to fix the problem, and all the things you will try to do once you leave to make the illness go away. You control the time to the extent that the doctor has no space to do or say anything. Then you leave without getting the expert opinion from the one person who can solve your problem. This happens all because you insist on striving toward finding a solution in your own power. You gave no room for the doctor to act or direct. Instead, God wants us to stand still and hold our peace. This means physically being still and mentally holding onto peace, not allowing stress, overwhelm, and anxiety to consume our minds and hearts.

Look at another instance in which God tells His people to stand still, allowing Him to work and make His will be done in 2 Chronicles 20:17: "You will not need to fight in this battle. *Position yourselves, stand still* and see the salvation of the LORD, who is with you, O Judah and Jerusalem!" (emphasis added).

In this passage, we are reminded that we do have a positional role to fill. It is not that we should give up all activities and let God do everything. He tells us that we are to take a position, to be where we are supposed to be considering the situation at hand, and then simply stand still. From a healing standpoint, this "position" means surrendering to the truth that we are merely human, and that God is God. There are limits to what we can humanly accomplish toward our objective of pursuing wholeness and emotional health. When we reach that limit, our position needs to resemble one of expectation of healing but also recognition that God will do the work. We position ourselves to receive that healing by knowing the certainty of it and then standing still while God does the work.

In the Psalms, we see more support for stillness as a position for God to operate: "Meditate within your heart on your bed, and be still. Selah." (4:4)

In the gospels, we see Jesus commanding the wind and storm to cease:

> Then He arose and rebuked the wind, and said to
> the sea, "Peace, be still!" And the wind ceased
> and there was a great calm. But he said to them,

"Why are you so fearful? How is it that you have no faith?" (Mark 4:39-40)

In this passage, we see a metaphor for internal struggles and the storms of life. We can command peace in our frantic minds and for them to be still rather than allowing fear and lack of faith to creep in. In reality, we do get tossed around by the events of life, and we do get scared at times. In our panic, we can call out to Him and ask Him to help us be peaceful and still. When we do that, the storms disappear.

We find perhaps the most powerful passage in the Bible demonstrating how much God wants us to be still and know Him in Luke:

> Now it happened as they went that He entered a certain village; and a certain woman named Martha welcomed Him into her house. And she had a sister called Mary, who also sat at Jesus' feet and heard His Word. But Martha was distracted with much serving, and she approached Him and said, "Lord, do You not care that my sister has left me to serve alone? Therefore tell her to help me." And Jesus answered and said to her, "Martha, Martha, you are worried and troubled about many things. But one thing is needed, and Mary has chosen that good part, which will not be taken away from her." (10:38-42)

Mary sat at Jesus' feet and heard His Word. By implication, we understand that she was being still and listening. She was not bustling about and striving to do anything. In her stillness, she was positioned to know her Lord because she was able to listen to him. She was in a receptive state of stillness. If she had been caught up in Martha's motions, she would have been too distracted to know her Lord.

When we keep our stillness, when we keep our mental and physical peace and calm, only then can we know He is God. There are several other verses that speak to the importance of peace and calm, which are components of stillness:

And let the peace of God rule in your hearts, to which also you were called in one body; and be thankful. (Col 3:15)

You will keep him in perfect peace, whose mind is stayed on You, because he trusts in You. (Isa 26:3) (As an aside related to this verse, neuropsychological research has shown us that the human brain can only focus on one thing at a time. This verse confirms that if we focus on God, it will bring about peace. It is not possible to think about God and think about your struggles at the exact same time. Turning our attention to God requires stilling all the other competing thoughts in our minds.)

These things I have spoken to you, that in Me [Jesus] you may have peace. In the world you will have tribulation; but be of good cheer, I have overcome the world. (John 16:33)

Stillness incorporates calmness and peace. We find these in Christ, as He tells us. But there is even more to know about God's command of *raphah*. Its meaning goes beyond peace and calm. You can discover this by again uncovering the original language used to write these verses. In the Greek, the phrase "have peace" is the word "*eirene*." According to Strong's Concordance, this word means "a state of national tranquility, peace between individuals, security, safety, prosperity." In Isaiah, the Hebrew word for peace is "*shalowm*," meaning completeness, soundness, welfare, tranquility, contentment." But God did not tell us to have peace and know that He is God. He told us to be still. He used very different words, so we know that stillness, having components of peace and calm, comprises a much broader meaning.

A few weeks ago, I was watching a nature program on television that showed a leopard hunting its prey, a classic scene in nature programming. This time, though, what grabbed my attention was the movements and posture of the leopard as he stalked the antelope.

The leopard moved closer to the antelope in slow and controlled movements. He kept his eyes on the antelope and in deliberate movements, he inched toward his prey. Then when the leopard reached a certain point, he stopped. He held his stance in absolute, complete stillness. The only muscles I could see moving were around his lungs. What a remarkable ability to hold a physical position as rigid as a statue for any length of time!

What struck me was that, despite his physical stillness, this creature was highly alert and 100 percent engaged in targeting the antelope. Nothing about this scene conveyed a sense of "peace" or "calm," even though he was completely still.

Why is this important for you? I want you to know that you can be physically still – maybe even be completely silent and be in a quiet environment – but have a whirling, active, unsettled, or even cluttered mind. You might be in an "alert-mode," which I find myself in at times. I seem to be scanning my environment, looking for some vague, undefined situation. My body can be still, but my mind can still be active.

Within the definition of *raphah* is another series of concepts that will help you grasp even more deeply the exact posture God wants us to take. Beyond the idea of ceasing striving, *raphah* also means to drop down, to lower, to leave alone, to show one's self slack and weak.

In God's directive to be still, He certainly wants us to stop striving but also to understand the positional relationship we have with him. We realize that we are lower, that we need to "drop down" and leave things alone. He even wants us to be weak! We are to dial back and stop trying, which indeed reveals our relative weakness compared to the power of God. In His stillness, He means for us to lower our defenses, both physical and emotional. In our weakness, He strength is made perfect (2 Cor 12:9). When we deliberately bring ourselves down and connect with our weakness, only then can we know that He is God.

This is what stillness is. Certainly, it consists of not moving physically. But, mentally, it also means taking the posture of a quiet mind without the chatter and commotion that often occupies our brains. Think of still waters, as in the 23rd Psalm. The waters He leads us by are not raging, they are not churned up, nor are they stagnant. They are still, and they represent a resting place.

In *raphah* stillness, God wants us to stop all activity at all levels, and humbly lower ourselves as we stop attempting to control everything. This is not an empty mind, nor is it an altered state of consciousness as in hypnosis. Rather, it represents a postural stance in which we realize and acknowledge the following: "I know nothing" (compared to the all-knowing God of the universe).

"I can do nothing" (apart from God's working through us; see John 15:5b, "for without Me you can do nothing").

"I can be nothing," (apart from the saving grace of God, see Gal 6:3, "For if anyone thinks himself to be something, when he is nothing, he deceives himself," and John 1:3, "All things were made through Him, and without Him nothing was made that was made.").

Picture yourself in this highly humbling and almost intimidating place – deep acknowledgment that we are vulnerable and completely insufficient without Him. That is the place of being still in which God can then show up mightily.

We are surrendered, in submission to the Ultimate Authority of the entire universe in peace, calm, and stillness. We have the certainty of knowing with complete confidence that the One who is in charge is actually in charge. We surrender to the reality that God knows things that we do not know, and in fact, we cannot know. This act of submission can feel unnerving, and even scary, for those who have control or trust issues. Acknowledging our place relative to the omniscient, omnipotent, and omnipresent God removes "us" as the one in control. Over time, as you practice stillness and press more deeply into understanding God's character, this position will bring you comfort and hope. But for some, this initially will feel threatening: "If I am not doing something or actively controlling my life, then who is?"

I understand this mindset very well, as I also used to have these scary thoughts. If I dial myself back, then who will make things happen? Who will take control? If I am supposed to let God control things, what does that even look like? How do things happen if I do not make them happen?

These fear-based questions went through my mind and made me resist giving control over to God. Because I could not understand something, it was tough for me to fully surrender. If God is not physically beside me, how can He cause circumstances to happen or situations to change?

During my fasting experience, the most important thing I did was to fully surrender to God, allowing Him to have His way with me because He told me that is what He wanted. I then faced a choice. Do I submit, be still, and take a risk of "nothing happening because I am not making it happen?" Or do I push through and still operate in my own power, essentially shutting out God's voice in certain areas?

For a Type-A personality, this was a tough decision! But I was serious about needing answers and wanting to move forward in my life. So I took a chance and allowed myself to be in *raphah* stillness. In my situation, this meant no more marketing activities for my business, no more actively trying to get new clients, and no longer doing the day-to-day operations that normally consumed my time. Talk about a challenge! When I stripped all those things away, I found that I did not even know what to do with myself. Being still not only felt vulnerable, it felt disorienting. What, exactly, do I do with time each day?

I did continue with my current clients and the household duties. But as for the "extra stuff," I learned to open my Bible more frequently through the day and how to pray more powerfully at times I did not normally pray.

Guess what happened? Not only was God able to heal my wounds and reveal things to me I did not know, but He also took care of my finances. Out of the blue, three new clients approached me in one week. None of them came from sources I expected, nor did I ever meet them prior to them reaching out to me for coaching. And that, my friends, is how God works when we give up the perception of control and let Him steer the ships of our lives. Our role is obedience and to say, "Yes, Lord," when He speaks. Supernaturally, things appear and move us forward.

I often wonder if people who pray to God for healing do not get the answers they seek because they are hyper-focused on what *they* want. Sometimes, as in my situation, God wants to address something within us first before He answers the questions and concerns in our minds. Yet if we never allow stillness, we cannot hear Him trying to get through to us. We have our own agendas. Yes, God cares about our agendas, especially if they are in alignment with His will for our lives. But oftentimes He needs to heal something in us first, or prompt us toward forgiveness or repentance before He can release the things we pray for.

I started my fast because I wanted answers about a particular matter. But God wanted His way with me first. Only when I allowed that to happen was I able to more fully emerge in His purpose for my life. I had to open myself up to what He wanted to tell me, even if I did not understand how it related to my personal agenda. Talk about risky! To me, it felt really scary. But I am so grateful every day for that experience because it has removed obstacles I did not know existed. That is what happens when we pursue even the things we know God put on our hearts. We exhibit "the Abrahamic syndrome." God gives us a vision, and we say, "OK, God, I'll take it from here" and pursue our version of what we think God wants us to do.

Although this section of the book is about the spiritual basis of stillness, I inserted my personal experience here because I know some readers will have similar thoughts about the concept of submission and surrender. In our worldly system, the idea of submission is generally negative. It implies vulnerability and a sense of wrongness. We do not like the concept of submission because it feels like we also embrace the idea of another person controlling us or having substantial power over us. It seems like we become willing slaves to someone or something else if we submit to that entity.

The fear or resistance to submission to God, however, confuses God with people. Many people falsely believe that submitting to God is the same thing as submitting to a person, or group of people, who may seem strange or weird (specifically, Christians). Often Christians come across as silly, or as if they believe a myth. And submitting to God is essentially admitting that these "strange" people are right and admitting that you are wrong. That feels discouraging and victimizing.

Please know that in submitting to God, you are not submitting to another person, you are not making yourself vulnerable to being hurt or shamed, nor are you susceptible to being damaged or taken advantage of. No, in fact, you are in the safest place you could possibly imagine. That place is within the will and presence of God Almighty, the One whose breath is in your lungs, the One who is true, faithful, and just. Submission to Him is not submitting to people, even other Christians, who may have presented a false or incomplete understanding of Him.

In stillness, you submit and surrender to the one thing in the entire universe you can fully trust and rely upon. Yes, bad things have happened to you. People may have victimized you in the past, you may have had serious injustices done to you, or you may have had accidents that permanently altered the course of your life.

Unfortunately, in this world, bad things will always happen. We live in a fallen reality in which people and worldly systems will disappoint you. This is the base condition of humanity.

But God is not of this world. His will is not in alignment with the will of the enemy who dominates the earthly existence. Luckily, we have God's Word to rely on and to use as our guiding light to give us hope for a better future, and an assured eternity with the One who loves us....and YOU! He can give us assurance and direction when we feel lost and confused. It is Him we can trust with our submission and surrender, not another human who could likely let us down. In fact, God is the only One we can fully and completely trust to never give up on us. God will never let us down! He cannot. Disappointment is not within His character. When we perceive that He "failed," we are wrong. He did not fail. People failed us. Our only hope for answers, perspective, and certainty of justice is to consult Him and then be still.

In *raphah* stillness, we cease striving, we cease running, we cease distracting ourselves and trying to make ourselves feel better by attempting to control, or by getting overwhelmed by circumstances. Yet at the same time, we are calm and peaceful, and therefore open and receptive to see and hear God, indeed, to KNOW God. This is what the verse says – when we position ourselves within *raphah* stillness, we will know He is God.

Look at Psalm 46:10 again: "Be still, and know that I am GOD." The Psalmist uses the conjunction "and." This shows that when we are still, we WILL know God. Be still, AND know He is God. It is when we reach this *raphah* state of stillness that we reach the end of ourselves and turn ourselves over to the One who made us in our mothers' wombs, who knew us before the foundation of the world, and who has our names written on the palm of His hand.

That is the God who will speak to you, give you direction and guidance, and HEAL your broken heart. When we achieve *raphah* stillness, we know for a fact who WE are, and who GOD is. This is why God tells us to "be still."

Now that you understand the spiritual meaning of stillness, via the original language in which God communicated this truth, let us turn to the psychological explanation of stillness.

The Psychology of Stillness

You probably know that traditional mental health research and therapies do not incorporate Christian doctrine or ideas. When I describe the psychology of stillness, I will sort through the blatantly non-Christian aspects. This does not leave too much left to describe, unfortunately. In the secular pursuit of finding ways to reduce anxiety and stress, and enhance stillness and calm, the mental health field has fully embraced the Buddhist method of meditation. It is considered a standard aspect of the treatment of anxiety and other mood disorders. While various forms of non-Christian meditation exist, they all have one concept in common: the elevation of the "self" as the ultimate source of knowledge and power.

In some forms of meditation, the person is encouraged to "empty" their minds. In other forms, they are directed to "connect with the universe." Many therapists attend continuing education training programs to learn how to teach their clients to use these strategies, primarily to reduce anxiety, stress, and overwhelm.

In fact, numerous research studies show this to be accurate – regularly practicing this type of meditation can have an immediate effect of lowering stress and anxiety. Used over time, some studies have shown that using meditation techniques can have as strong an impact as using anti-anxiety medications. This sounds very impressive. In no way do I want to diminish or deflect from true improvements in symptoms that many have experienced using meditation.

However, as a Christ follower and a person who takes the Bible seriously, I recognize a massive problem in promoting Buddhist meditation, or any other kind of meditation that does not have Christ as the center. That problem is that the person meditating, especially if he or she "empties" his or her mind, has no idea what supernatural entities have been granted access to the mind and soul. I reflect on the data of the rapidly expanding epidemic of mental health problems in the western world, and I wonder how the reliance on secular methods over the past 30 years in particular may have inadvertently contributed to the problem.

The reality is that evil exists. Satan is real, and he has his followers. If you have never studied the role of Satan and his realm and objectives, you will find a short introduction to evil as described in the Bible in chapter six. We have an enemy and he has followers.

In the supernatural realm, these demonic forces look for opportunities to influence people.

When we "empty" our minds, we become vulnerable to just about any spiritual entity that might want to impact us. With an empty or disengaged mind, we lack the ability to exercise discernment and test the spirits we may be encountering. The same issue happens when a person "connects with the universe." The concept of "the universe" is new age, and therefore based in an anti-Christ or pagan spirit. When a person connects in that realm and lacks the grounding knowledge of Scripture, that person has no way of knowing with "what" they are connecting.

For some people, this concept can seem spooky or even unbelievable. We are not given a spirit of fear, so I urge you to quell any sense of apprehension, hesitation, or panic if you are not accustomed to thinking about the spiritual realm. I only bring it up here (without first laying the groundwork for the reality of demons and evil spirits) because it is very relevant to the psychological understanding of "stillness."

If you have ever consulted a secular psychologist who taught you these techniques, please do not panic or get concerned! The fact that you have Christ in your heart gives you a significant measure of spiritual protection that non-Christians lack. I suggest that you pray to God about your experience and see if the Holy Spirit convicts you about anything. I have never personally worked with any Christ follower who had significant problems stemming from the practice of Buddhist meditation. But I have seen non-Christians who clearly manifest signs of darkness. For Christians, the main concern is exposing yourself to an evil entity that deceives you into believing something that is not true.

For instance, during meditation, people report seeing human-like entities. These entities may not always have the best intentions. But within the Buddhist tradition, evil does not exist. Therefore, according to this worldview, any entity you encounter will always have your best interests at heart. This simply goes against what God tells us in the Bible. In fact, evil DOES exist, it has a leader (Satan), and he comes to kill, steal, and destroy (as Jesus Himself tells us in John 10:10). You will read more about this later, but for now, just know that a supernatural world does exist, it is possible to interact with it, and not everything in that realm is godly.

Although this use of Buddhist techniques is worrisome, there are other aspects of the psychology of stillness that more closely align with Scripture. One technique is mindfulness. In mindfulness, the person develops a higher degree of control over where he puts his attention. The person is guided to stop thinking about the past or the future, but instead focus on the here and now. Jesus told us, "Do not worry about tomorrow" (Matt 6:34) after listing off all the things we are NOT supposed to think about (specifically, where we will get our food or clothes).

An effective technique to help force our attention away from worrisome and unproductive thoughts is to instead turn our focus to the present moment. This describes the essence of mindfulness – it is the deliberate practice of "being" in the present moment. You can achieve this relatively easily, which makes mindfulness even more attractive. You simply turn your attention to what you are experiencing with your five senses.

For example, right now if you look up from this page, notice all the things you can see. What objects do you see? What colors do you notice? What shapes surround you? Are there areas in the shadows and some in light? Do you see different shades?

Then turn your attention to your auditory sense. What do you hear? Can you detect all the background noises or sounds? Do you hear humming from appliances if you are inside your house? Do you hear the sounds of nature? Can you determine what they are?

What smells or aromas do you perceive? Do you notice many of them, or relatively few?

What can you feel? Can you notice the pressure of your clothing on your skin? What is the sensation of your body against the chair you sit in right now? What about the air temperature – is it cool, warm, or just right? Is there a breeze? Is it moving the hair on your head, or your clothing, or anything around you?

If you are eating something, what does it taste like? Focus on the flavor or the combination of flavors. What does the pressure of the food feel like in your mouth?

I hope you are starting to understand what mindfulness is. It is the exclusive focus on the here and now, the present moment and all the sensations and experiences of this moment. So much happens when we become more mindful. This process forces us away from worry and judgment and fear. It pulls us out of our anxieties and into the reality of the present moment. From this position, we can see how "big" life is! It shows you clearly what we miss when we zoom past life mindlessly and with our heads buried in our smartphones. At any given moment, we can notice and experience a huge range of things. God's creation is enormous, and we can more powerfully experience it by refusing to give our attention over to things that entertain, distract, or disengage us from His creation.

One of the most calming aspects of practicing mindfulness is that it pulls us out of anxiety, worry, and stress. We realign with the truth of right now – that God is sovereign, He is in control, He is always here to support you, comfort you, and guide you. Mindfully focusing on God's creation using the senses He gave us transports us away from emotions that can deceive or distract us. We become more grounded in God through this technique.

Even though mindfulness stems from a secular perspective, it does conform to Scripture and is a relatively easy way to begin the process of being still. Mindfulness is not the same as stillness because our minds are still active and searching. Mindfulness teaches us how much control we have over our thoughts and even our emotions. Give it a try. At first, it may feel awkward and you might find yourself feeling fidgety, or even anxious.

Our modern lifestyle has trained our brains to crave, and search for, some outside stimulus to capture and keep our attention. The use of smartphones and mobile devices exploits the parts of our brains that are highly attracted to new stimuli. In fact, I have noticed over the last 10 years that more and more adults are declaring that they have "adult ADD." This is simply not true. Attention Deficit Disorder (ADD) is a neurological condition from childhood. If you did not have it as a child, then you did not develop it as an adult. It simply does not work that way.

The excessive use of mobile devices has given you the illusion that you cannot sustain your attention. Mobile devices have trained us to only hold attention on something for a maximum of two to seven minutes. Most viral videos or engaging posts on the internet last around two minutes. If there is a video blog, it will typically last no more than seven minutes.

Research into the impact of the internet has shown that these time frames are the most frequent for online engagement. The next time you pick up your phone to check social media, take a moment to evaluate how long your attention stays on one thing (especially videos). This is a startling exercise for most people. After two minutes, you may find your mind wandering, or you might experience a "need" to keep scrolling or to find something else to capture your attention.

Physical structures in our brains change based on what we require of them. God created us with free will, and with that gift of free will, we have a brain that accommodates our choices. If we feed the part of our brain that craves new stimuli, new visual images, and only brief headlines to "understand" world complexities, our brains will essentially say, "OK, let's change to start absorbing information in this other way."

Then the newer brain structures that we insisted on creating activate when something we are watching or listening to feels old or stale. We trained our brains to sustain attention for maybe two minutes, so after that amount of time, the brain sends signals of boredom. With that boredom might also come a bit of anxiety or tension, fueling a need to find something new that is interesting and engaging.

Think about what happens to your emotions and your thoughts as you engage with social media. I will use Facebook as an example, but any internet site can create this same experience.

As you log onto your Facebook app, you immediately see a picture and words. The visual impact you notice is determined exclusively by what Facebook has decided you will see when you log on. For many people, it might be something pleasant – a picture of your friend doing something fun or of their children accomplishing some feat. You have an emotional response to this, most probably a positive emotion. Then you start to scroll after viewing the picture and accompanying verbal description. As you scroll, you might notice someone shared a GoFundMe page for someone they know who had a horrible event happen to them and now they are desperately in need of money. This evokes a range of responses from intense sympathy, to pity, to confusion, or even guilt if you decide not to contribute. You may briefly – meaning in less than 15 seconds – mentally debate about what to do and feel about this fundraising campaign. You make a decision and continue scrolling.

Next, you see a political post. You may experience a jolt of righteous indignation or disgust at the so-and-sos on the other end of the political spectrum, or elation at the outcome of a recent political circumstance. You react with an emoji or even leave a brief comment under the post.

And you keep scrolling.....

You then see a funny video that causes you to stop scrolling for about two minutes as you watch a very amusing situation play out on your phone. You may chuckle softly to yourself. Then you keep scrolling and you see a meme with a beautiful background photo, over which is written a motivating statement designed to help you feel more energized to go out and conquer the rest of your day. You keep scrolling and now you see another meme with a Bible verse that momentarily encourages you and reminds you to pray for a situation in your life.

You keep scrolling and then see an ad for something you had been researching online. It reminds you that you want to purchase that item, but you do not have time right now. Next, you see that someone you do not know in real life, but have somehow connected with on Facebook, has broken her ankle and now requires surgery. You react with a sad emoji because you have sympathy for anyone going through that painful circumstance.

All of this happens in five to ten minutes. Look back and see how your emotions have swung rapidly and drastically from one intense experience to another. Even more concerning, you probably cannot remember each Facebook post you saw during those five minutes, even though each one caused you to feel an emotion and a possible connection with another person or situation.

When you put your smartphone away after this quick check-in with Facebook, your phone might be physically out of sight, but your brain remains in the mode of requiring outside stimuli to keep your mind active and interested. You now try to reengage with your life, but your brain is still attached to needing the screen on your phone to create that engagement.

What happens next? You scan your environment to reorient your brain about your physical location. Then you spend a few seconds figuring out your next move and what you will accomplish next. The problem is that you forced your brain to go on a wild roller coaster of emotions and judgments of situations based on only fragments or small pieces of information.

As you reengage in your real-life events, your brain still needs to move on from one thing to the next thing quickly. This means it feels hard to concentrate on one item or task, and some people experience this as anxiety and unsettledness. You may start to feel jittery or nervous, not quite knowing why. But you know the one thing that will help you feel calmer – checking Facebook! It will put your brain into a very passive mode of alternating between intense emotions so that you do not have to do the "hard work" of finding a task, focusing on it for a long period, and then completing it.

Amid all this brain tumult, you also expend a tremendous amount of energy. Each time you have an emotional response, an energy response comes with it. When our feelings constantly move up and down, we discharge precious emotional and physical energy that is then unavailable for other tasks. For instance, if you are trying to lose weight by resisting sugary items, and you spend your day allowing your brain to be a passive consumer of emotionally charged social media, you simply will not have enough energy (or what you may know as "willpower") to resist that batch of cookies on your counter. If you have committed to getting your budget under control, directing your energies toward constantly changing stimuli means that as you drive past your favorite shoe store, you have less willpower to draw upon for avoiding the temptation of impulse purchases.

Hopefully, you can understand the uphill battle you will wage as you seek to be still. Everything in modern life revolves around the complete opposite of stillness. You absolutely can achieve stillness, though. I do not want you to feel discouraged!

The reason I described all of this is so you realize that your initial attempts at being still may be frustrating. You may experience anxiety or inner tension, plus a strong desire to have something to specifically think about or direct your attention to. This is a normal reaction for most people. It just means you must put some time, space, and effort into retraining your brain to be still. There are steps you can take to make the process easier, and I will discuss those in chapter nine. But you must be willing to continue to grow your "stillness muscles," that part of your mind that requires rest and proper positioning before the God of the universe.

He knows what you are up against, and He knows the forces that have worked to keep you away from stillness and instead toward busyness and distractions. But He does want you to keep pursuing Him in the way He has established the pursuit: to be still and know that He is God.

You might be able to appreciate how the practice of mindfulness can assist in your stillness quest. You will learn more as we go along, but always remember that for most people, stillness does not happen instantly, or even easily. It takes time to develop and mature. Extend yourself some mercy and grace to allow the time it takes to learn how to be still.

Why, from a psychological standpoint, is stillness important? According to psychological research, we know that the opposite of stillness – meaning noisy, crowded, and busy environments – has dramatic impacts at many levels of human experience. In the 1970s, researchers discovered that subway noise had a direct, harmful impact on children's learning ability. More research has shown chronic noise is associated with decreasing children's health and slower cognitive and language development. This culminates in lower reading scores among children who live in more noisy areas.

Noise can lead to high blood pressure and heart disease, in addition to chronic stress. High stress means your body is flooded with cortisol, a stress hormone that makes it harder to lose weight. Of course, loud noise can cause hearing problems, but it also causes us to tune out speech as a way of coping with noisy environments. Thus, talking becomes part of the background noise that is avoided, we pay less attention to other people, and our brains fail to develop ways of understanding speech. You can see how massive communication problems stem from this, and it could help explain why people who live in crowded cities can move about seemingly unaware of other people around them. What happens, though, when someone needs help or is calling you to get your attention? If our brains develop ways of ignoring sounds, all kinds of sounds simply blend together.

In contrast, more recent research shows that extended periods of silence lead to the growth of new brain cells in the area of the brain responsible for learning and memory. Scientists are discovering that silence – a component of stillness – actually allows the brain to better and more effectively process information. Constantly bombarding the brain with stimuli deprives the brain of the time and space it requires to pull together the information already in the brain, move it to long-term memory storage, and actually think things through.

Much like sleep, the brain can only perform certain tasks that enhance problem-solving, creativity, learning, and memory when it

Page | 64

has enough time of sustained silence. Keeping our minds active and stimulated with constantly changing images, sounds, and thoughts prevent the brain from doing the one thing we want it to do best – that is to THINK!

The process of thinking happens most properly during stillness. Pumping more information into the brain keeps it in high-alert mode. Constantly inputting huge amounts of data forces the brain to rapidly process what is coming into it, whether the brain is capable of processing it or not. This means that most of what comes into our brains is lost. We are so inundated with stimuli that our brains fail to recognize, ingest, and process that information.

However, being silent and still allows the brain time to absorb pieces of information, process them, relate them to information already in the brain, and then come to conclusions or solutions. Our minds can expand and begin to process and internalize when we cut off the stimuli. Incoming information from the world causes our brains to contract as it tries to react and input that new data. This means your mind constricts as it tries to focus and narrow down the information. But brain contraction restricts creativity and the ability to make connections between ideas.

Whenever I go on vacation for a week, I make a concerted effort not to think too much about work, my clients, or my retreat and conference development. Instead, I focus on enjoying the locations we visit, being mindful of my surroundings, and simply loving the time with my family. Invariably, I return to work the next week not only physically energized, but also with new ideas and plans. When we allow our minds to rest from the day-to-day stuff that consumes our attention, our subconscious mind can go to work. Under the radar, our minds synthesize information and can more fully access other memories, experiences, ideas, and thoughts that have been stored in our brains. This results in better ideas and plans when we return to our normal lives. But do not wait until you go on vacation to achieve this! Learn and practice being still on a regular basis and you are likely to have this happen to you too.

In addition to the cognitive benefits of stillness and quiet, they are also associated with positive changes in your physical health. Less noise and commotion make blood pressure and heart rate decrease. Our bodies release muscle tension and stress. The veins in our cardiovascular system relax and allow more blood flow to our extremities, such as our fingers and toes. When we experience stress, our veins contract and restrict blood flow to those extremities. If your hands get cold when you are overwhelmed or stressed, it is because of this process. It is where the term "cold, clammy hands" come from, and it happens because of reduced blood flow. The clammy part happens because we tend to sweat more when we are alert and tense.

Stillness reverses all of those physical reactions to stress. As our bodies physically relax, our minds can focus on what is inside of them already, which enhances learning and memory. We have time to evaluate and consider the experiences we have had, to put them into perspective and draw more lessons from them. The ideas, thoughts, fantasies, wishes, and memories can surface, allowing opportunities to explore them more deeply, at both the conscious and unconscious levels.

As you can see, there are both spiritual and psychological reasons why *raphah* stillness is something God wants for us, and we can understand it encompasses far more than simply physical stillness or silence.

This chapter describes how stillness, and related concepts like silence, quiet, and submission, are defined and help us connect with God. It also underscores why we sometimes resist being still. Being still is a choice, and it is entirely within our power and our will to surrender ourselves in this way. Please know that God will never violate your free will. If you hesitate and resist His desire, He will allow you the opportunity to pursue that path.

But there are forces that seek to prevent you from being still. You can recognize these forces by understanding the opposite of stillness. Mental chatter, busyness, striving, anxiety, worry, overwhelm, and impulsivity have no place in stillness, yet many of these experiences dominate our day-to-day existence. You end up exhausted by the ping-ponging of your energy and attention all day long, which only makes you more vulnerable to life situations overwhelming you. When you live on the edge, only a small shove pushes you over.

All these anti-stillness forces lead you to higher levels of emotional distress. You start to search for ways to feel better, to make these tough feelings go away as quickly and easily as possible (because in our modern society, ONLY things that are quick and easy are acceptable options). What happens? In our efforts to escape the craziness in our minds, we veer toward fixes – distracting ourselves with mindless internet scrolling, munching on snacks that lack nutritional value, overeating, wine and alcohol, pornography, and even drugs.

These coping mechanisms prevent you from deeply engaging not only with others but also ourselves. We end up unaware of what drives us, what motivates us, and what our true priorities are. Our own behavior feels mysterious, out of our control, and therefore uncontrollable. The enemy is a deceiver, and he is good at it. He influences you to stay in a state of constant mental motion and commotion, lulling you into believing the lies he feeds you about yourself and God. If the enemy succeeds in keeping us distracted by what he wants us to do, see, and feel, then that keeps us farther from God.

God says, "Be still." The enemy says, "But it feels hard, and it is easier to pour a glass or two (or three) of wine and let the internet dictate what I think." Stillness leads to God and His kingdom. Mental busyness leads to Satan and his dominion.

Will it be hard to train your mind and body to be still? Probably. Is it worth it? Definitely. Why is it worth it? Because when we are still, we will know that He is God. This begs the next logical question: What does it mean to KNOW God? Let's find out.

What Does It Mean to "Know" God?

God tells us that when we are still, we can know Him. You may think you know Him, but I suggest that if you walk around with emotional strongholds, there are deeper levels of Him to know and embrace. We can begin the discovery process by again examining the Hebrew meaning of the word, "know," in Psalm 46:10.

The Hebrew word used in this Psalm is *yada*, which means "to recognize, to understand" (Strong's concordance #3045). However, this particular Hebrew word has an additional layer of meaning beyond the straightforward idea of understanding something at an intellectual level. In fact, *yada* suggests a far more intimate, deep, experiential understanding of someone or something.

Yada is used in other places in Scripture to suggest the deepest, most profound way of engaging with someone else. In Genesis 4:1, 17, and 25, we read, "Now Adam knew [*yada*} his wife, and she conceived and bore Cain…..and Cain knew [*yada*] his wife…..And Adam knew [*yada*] his wife again, and she bore a son…."

While this implies a sexual, or at least carnal, meaning of the word "knew/know," the Hebrew word actually suggests a certain and intimate way of understanding. There is a sense of dedication to someone so we can engage with them at the most meaningful levels. It also means to make one's self known, so there is the idea of exposing one's self to another and allowing one's self to be known by another.

Yada has such a complex, textured meaning! It goes beyond the understanding of a simple fact and instead elevates the connection between individual entities. God is telling us that by being still, we can have an intimate, deep, certain, and true recognition of the fullness of who He is.

In being still, we drop our defenses and our pretenses, and we fully and intimately immerse ourselves into the reality of who God is. He is all-knowing, all-loving, all-present, unchanging, compassionate, and just. We can, through stillness, absorb this truth. In doing so, we open ourselves up to receiving what He has to give, including emotional healing. We can more completely rely on Him without feeling vulnerable to a threat of any kind.

Some readers will start to feel excited at the prospect of encountering God in this way. You may be one of those readers and are ready to learn the steps to make this happen.

Others of you, however, might be experiencing a range of unpleasant reactions. You may feel scared, resistant, and quite reluctant to have this kind of intimate knowledge of God. Or perhaps there is a part of you that feels anger or resentment as you consider growing closer to God.

In working with hundreds of people in recent years, I know that many people have these reactions. The reasons for the reactions vary greatly. You may have a personal history of abuse or neglect that made you question why God did not save you or why He allowed it to happen, or you doubted He was even there during those horrendous times. From these beliefs about God, you may have developed anger toward Him or doubt that He really does want to heal you. You may know the promises of Scripture for your healing and wholeness, but you doubt they apply to you personally.

Or perhaps you are scared about what will happen when you let down your guard, be still, and allow yourself to fully know God. Do

Page | 68

you feel ashamed to be in front of him? Are you self-conscious and concerned that He will chastise you or condemn you? It is very common for people to fail to fully comprehend His grace, and that He DOES forgive your sins when you accept His Son, Jesus Christ, as your savior. In Christ, your sins are as far from you as the East is from the West (Ps 103:12). This means that He not only knows what you have done in the past, but He also has *completely forgiven you!* You have been made as white as snow as long as you are covered by the blood of His Son.

Paul tells us in Romans that there is no condemnation in Christ (8:1). Let me repeat: There is NO condemnation in Christ. I will reiterate: There is NO CONDEMNATION in Christ! If any part of you hesitates to access the fullness of God because you think He will make you feel guilty, ashamed, or rejected because of anything you have done in the past, PLEASE take five minutes to meditate upon the truth of Romans 8:1. Do not read any farther until you allow the reality to settle in that He will NOT condemn you in any way.

If you ever hear condemning voices in your mind, rest assured that they are not from God. How do I know? Because there is NO CONDEMNATION in Christ. If you tell yourself that you are too dirty, unworthy, bad, unlovable, or have a "but you don't know what I've done and how much I've screwed up" attitude, I beg you to take some time to study the concept of grace. The whole point of Christ is that we ALL have screwed up, and none of us can save ourselves or make ourselves presentable before the Creator of the Universe. Paul killed Christians. Peter denied Christ three times before His crucifixion. Christ not only accepted them, but He used them mightily for God's kingdom.

Believing that you did something so bad, or that something was done to you that made you unacceptable before God, completely negates the saving sacrifice of the cross. Trust in Him. Our lives here on earth can be nothing except far from perfect. But God provides a safe haven, a hope, and a light to a path forward with the promise of everything being made right again according to His timeline. You serve a God of restoration, resurrection, reconciliation, and redemption. You have nothing to fear, and, in fact, can come boldly to the throne of grace so you can claim the mercy and grace you require to help you in your time of need (Heb 4:16).

As you come to His throne via stillness, you will know He is God. You will have a deep, profound, intimate, and immersive understanding of who He is. This *yada* knowledge of God helps the process of surrender feel easier and more comfortable. You are not yielding control of your life to some uninterested, limited power, or untrustworthy entity.

No. You submit to the one true God, the One who IS truth and love and light. Imagine immersing yourself in the fullness of His being. Imagine turning yourself over to Him completely. Imagine allowing the perfection of the One who is totally trustworthy and will never let you down to absorb all your hurts, sorrows, pains, and despair, and to heal your heart forever, because He knows you and loves you.

Could you yearn for anything more fully? Christ saved you and made you acceptable before God. Now it is time to KNOW Him, according to the *yada* meaning of the word. You will be safe, secure, and in full alignment with Him as Your sovereign. Then you will be in the position of being able to hear His still, small voice speaking to you with the gravitas of ultimate truth. Getting your positional relationship to God properly fixed puts you in a place to receive His blessings. He wants you to be still so you can know He is God, meaning you will know Him deeply. It is in obedience to his directive to be still that we access the depths of His reality and understand that He can bestow more of what He knows we need. Experiencing God only at a surface or intellectual level is unsatisfying and limited.

Matthew tells an interesting story about an encounter Jesus had with Peter early on in His earthly ministry. In chapter 5, Jesus gets into a boat that is in the shallows near the shore to teach the people who had come to see Him. We are told that He "asked him [Peter] to put out a little from the land" (v. 3). Jesus did His teaching from the shallow area. Then, when He finished his sermon, He asked Peter to "launch out into the deep and let down your nets for a catch" (v. 4). Initially, Peter resists, but he still obeys the request. When he relents, Scripture tells us that Peter "caught a great number of fish, and their net was breaking" (v. 6).

Where did the blessings happen for Peter? Out in the deep. In the shallow areas, the people could hear and receive the intellectual understanding of Jesus's teaching. But solving Peter's problem of not having caught any fish after toiling all night could only happen with his obedience to go out into the deep.

You probably know God intellectually. Each day, I encourage you to read His Word so you can get more and more of it into your mind and, ultimately, into your heart. But if you have resisted going deep with God, allowing yourself to be still and experience the *yada*, deep knowing of Him, you probably are not seeing as many blessings as you would hope.

Deep knowing of God requires stillness, a full and quiet surrender of your thoughts, feelings, worries, and pain. I know it can seem scary at first for the reasons I discussed earlier. But the truth is that only within this *yada* experience will He heal your emotional wounds.

But if God is perfect, and can heal us, how is it we became wounded in the first place? Where do emotional wounds originate, and why is understanding this important to our healing? Read on to learn about the root of the problem and why stillness is the path to healing.

Chapter Six: Understanding the Problem

For this people's heart has become calloused;
They hardly hear with their ears, And they have
closed their eyes. Otherwise they might see with
their eyes, hear with their ears, understand with
their hearts and turn, and I would heal them.
(Matt 13:15)

How Do We Get Emotionally Wounded?

Susan came into my office and gingerly sat down on the cushioned chair I had for my clients at the chronic pain center. She had just come from having an injection to help manage her back pain, and she wanted to speak with me quickly before she went home. This was unusual because people are typically not especially chatty after getting therapeutic injections. The treatments tend to be unpleasant, although effective.

As she settled in, she thanked me for seeing her at the last minute. She had been in therapy with me for about a year and a half. Many chronic pain patients (people with longstanding back pain, fibromyalgia, and migraines, for instance) experienced some sort of childhood trauma. The role of emotional experience in the perception of pain was an emerging field of study in psychology at that time. Patients often became defensive when their doctors referred them to see me, worried their doctors thought their pain was "all in their heads." Nothing was further from the truth. The physicians I worked with had a modern understanding of the complexity of pain and knew that emotions – especially emotions rooted in childhood trauma – play a key role in physical pain.

When Susan first came to see me, she was one of the defensive people. After a few weeks, however, she began to see the value in seeking psychotherapy, and we started making significant progress. About three months before, Susan revealed to me that her father had sexually molested her for years between the ages of about nine and sixteen. To complicate matters, her mother was an alcoholic, causing Susan to grow up in a chaotic, painful, and unsafe environment. To cope, she developed a mentality of hyper-control over her life. Everything had to be perfect. She believed it was her job and duty to "control" the feelings of everyone around her.

This excessive need to control her environment helped her mask the underlying terror of her life spiraling out of control. Growing up in such disorder, confusion, and hurt made her desperate to make sure she never experienced the level of emotional distress she endured as a child.

Susan's problems started emerging when she hurt her back doing some normal household chores one day. What began as a relatively minor event involving pulled muscles escalated over about a year into intense and diffuse lower back pain. The pain disturbed her sleep, made her unable to participate in the activities she and her husband loved to do throughout their 25 years of marriage, and culminated in her need to take daily, potent pain medication that came with its own bothersome side effects.

It took almost a year of psychotherapy for Susan to feel comfortable disclosing to me the details of her abuse. She carried enormous shame along with her deeply wounded heart. Muddying the waters, Susan felt guilty about resenting her father. In many ways, she harbored more anger toward her mother than her father – after all, her mother failed to protect her, and the alcoholism kept her disengaged from Susan.

But the issue that bothered Susan the most of all the hurts and trauma she endured as a child revolved around God. As a structurally religious family, Susan and her parents observed Lent and Susan's mother would give up alcohol for the entire 40 days. To Susan, this was devastating. How could her mother stay away from alcohol for God, but not for her? This kept Susan distant from God and resentful toward Him.

Childhood is brutal. As much as society and parenting have evolved to understanding the need to protect children from abusive situations, difficult and life-changing events happen to all of us. The range of what we each experience varies widely. But none of us can escape with a fully intact heart. We all get wounded – our parents disappoint us, they reject us, they fail to protect us, they neglect us, they transmit their own anxieties and wounds onto us, and sometimes they physically or verbally abuse us.

Naturally, we get wounded from other people around us as well. Our "friends" make fun of us, someone on the playground tells us, "You're ugly," or we do not get invited to someone's birthday party and it really hurts our feelings. These days, children and teens even have to deal with cyberbullying. In many ways, all the safeguards we have established to protect our children seem like a drop in the ocean with the myriad ways the internet and technology have opened up to inflict harm and emotional wounds. In extreme cases, cyberbullying has led to the suicides of young people. Of course, teachers, caregivers, church leaders, and neighbors also have the capacity to inflict emotional damage on a child. The sources of danger and potential negative influence seems limitless.

But perhaps, like me, you emerged from childhood relatively unscathed by abuse, bullying, or relentless teasing. Does this mean you have no wounds? Of course not! People in this situation develop emotional wounds with the accumulation of small, but regular, hurts that over time grow into bigger wounds – it is like "death by papercuts."

To help understand the range of sources of emotional pain, we will look at earthly causes and spiritual causes.

Earthly Causes of Emotional Wounds

This past summer, I had the pleasure of spending a day at a Florida beach with some friends and their four grandchildren. As a parent of grown children, it brings me joy to watch babies and toddlers play (it is so nice because I have no responsibility for entertaining them!). God used this ordinary event to show me other examples of how wounding happens all throughout childhood but in very subtle ways.

Among these four children, two of them were boys. The older boy made a sandcastle structure with a "sitting area" in it. I was impressed with his tenacity during construction. At the ripe age of 4, he had more of a work ethic than many adults I have known!

When he finished his castle, he called his younger brother over to play in it with him. The younger brother, however, had no interest in playing in the castle – he wanted to go back near the water. The older brother tried to "entice" (read: force) his brother to play by grabbing his hand and pulling him toward the castle.

The younger brother would have none of it. He pulled his hand away and yelled, "I don't want to play in your castle!" He was mean about this, and the older brother was crestfallen. You could see it on his face. Not only did his brother not want to play with him, but the older brother clearly felt *rejected*. A wound was inflicted right before my eyes.

This small moment in time showed me an important reality, and why it is folly to think that we "have it all together." Each of us has experienced small, seemingly insignificant moments where we interpret what happened as being rejected, excluded, belittled, not good enough, or discouraged. Imagine over the course of your lifetime how many times you experienced even a small event like this one. It adds up, and the smaller hurts build up to bigger hurts.

In reality, of course, you have experienced so many of these events that you cannot recall all of them. However, each one gets recorded in your subconscious and causes you to deploy a variety of coping and defense strategies to prevent yourself from feeling that hurt again. You will learn more about these in depth in a few chapters.

In my case, I grew up with wonderful, loving parents. I could not have asked for a more supportive, devoted, and caring mother and father team. They encouraged me and my brother to excel academically and (in the case of my athlete brother) physically as well. We lacked nothing and somehow emerged unspoiled and with a strong work ethic. My brother and I both have our doctorate degrees.

Despite this rather ideal scenario, our household was not perfect. High-achieving families (both of my parents have their doctorates) often go hand in hand with high anxiety. In fact, the level of anxiety felt thick at times, as if it had a physical presence.

This became a problem for me as a child. Anxiety means worry or uncertainty. Seeing my parents worried about things that they often could not control had a downstream impact on me. I grew up with my own sense of worry – "If my parents, who are adults and really smart, cannot protect themselves or me from the possible dangers of a big, scary world, then I had better make sure I am in control!"

I grew up, almost like Susan, with a high need to control things. If people "in charge" could not assure my safety, then I would do it myself. At its root laid the belief that I am vulnerable and the only way to be safe and protected is to work hard at it *myself*. This is one of my emotional wounds that I had no conscious idea about. God healed it during the period of fasting I described at the beginning of this book. But until that moment in which God made me see that I had a wounded heart, I assumed I had my act together. I mistakenly thought I was okay since I didn't have the horrific childhood that my therapy and coaching clients often had.

God taught me such a valuable, humbling lesson – none of us are free of wounding and believing lies about ourselves and God. We all fall short, and we all stray from God's will. None of us lack the need for a touch of healing from God, so He can correct the wrong things we believe. If you think you are somehow exempt from needing God's healing of some area of your life, then I invite you to study the stories in the Bible about pride. Start with Job, of course, but also focus on the story of the prodigal son, and the older son who remained with his father. The older son demonstrated pride that the father had to correct (Matt 15:28-31). The older son had received his portion of the father's property, but defensively complained that he "never disobeyed your orders" and "you never gave me even a young goat."

Even the most blessed among us fall prey to pride and beliefs that we are "good" and therefore deserve more blessings, or less suffering. This is not how it works. We can never be perfect. In our childhood are planted seeds of evil and deception. No amount of "good works" will erase the wrong thoughts in our heads and hearts that are in direct opposition to what God says.

I emphasize this point because I want you to understand that no matter what you grew up with – no matter what happened or did not happen to you – God's healing through Christ is available for everyone. Not only is it available, but it is also crucial that we leverage that healing. This is how we become more Christ-like. If we think we are "okay" because by all outward appearances we "have it all together," or that we are generally "good people," we operate in a spirit of pride. In that spirit, we fail to realize just how far we are from God's perfect goodness and how much we require Christ's finished work on the cross.

If you are a parent, then I want to tell you another aspect of earthly wounding that occurs, despite our best efforts to love and nurture our children. Children are born as highly self-centered beings. If you have had an infant, you know this to be true. Babies cry and vocally complain every time they have some type of irritation or discomfort, and they do not stop crying until that discomfort is gone. When they are hungry, you know about it. And you also know when their hunger is satisfied.

All babies only care about is themselves, and while it may seem silly to make such a statement, it is important to understand that it is true. If they were compliant and easy, the mother would never know when her baby needs something. Being insistent through crying communicates the baby's needs loudly and clearly.

Because a baby is born with a brain that is quite immature compared to an adult's brain, it makes sense that a baby lacks empathy toward an exhausted new mother who desperately needs a nap and a shower. The baby does not care because the baby cannot care. His or her brain is not developed to know anything beyond his or her physical sensations and how to communicate when he or she needs something.

As a baby moves through infancy, she develops an awareness that people exist other than just herself. She recognizes her parents and rewards them with smiles, coos, and laughter. However, despite the awareness, the baby still lacks empathy and remains able to only know about her own needs.

At the risk of making infancy like a caricature, the baby is in "all about me" mode. Empathy, caring, love, mutual respect, and restraint are higher-level brain operations that do not develop until later in childhood. Because of this, the "all about me" approach makes babies highly susceptible to feeling rejected.

At church one Sunday morning, I watched a young mother holding her infant, who was probably about seven or eight months old. Everyone was standing during the music portion of the service, and it was obvious that the mother was growing tired holding her son. She handed her son over to her husband, but the baby wanted his mother to continue holding him. He started to cry and reach out for the mother, but she just smiled at him and then looked away.

The baby continued to reach his arms to his mother, so the father tried to get his son's attention locked onto something else. This eventually worked and the baby quieted down and became interested in the toy the father was holding.

During this exchange, this baby was feeling rejected by his mother. The mother did absolutely nothing wrong and, in fact, probably saved herself from needing several chiropractor appointments the next week. It is completely reasonable for a mom to allow someone else to hold the baby.

But from the baby's self-centered point of view, he wanted his mother to hold him. He made every attempt to make it happen, but it did not. I could practically see the sense of rejection come over him. "Why doesn't my mommy want to hold me when I want her?" Each of us is primed to experience rejection from the earliest days of our lives. This is not rejection from someone that is meant to be unkind or hurtful. It stems from our built-in mentality of "only me," which sets the stage to experience hurt when something we want is withheld from us.

Over time, these little hurts compound. When the child is the target of a more intentional rejection, or painful words and actions from parents or other caregivers are leveled at the child, we already have a foundation of rejection. This foundation of rejection makes it even more hurtful when we realize that sometimes people we love or trust refuse us because they "choose" to refuse us.

As a parent, I know that sometimes I acted in ways that ended up causing my sons to feel as if I did not accept them for who they are. In fact, I have apologized to them for those times. I acted out of my own wounds and subsequent frustrations when I could not control certain things in them. Looking back, I wish I could re-do those moments. Of course, I cannot, but I serve a God of redemption and healing. I know that God will act in my boys as they approach the time to have their wounds healed.

While this is an earthly example, it becomes a wounding experience because we are each born under the spiritual influence of rejection. We end up feeling hurt and dejected because of natural life events that are not wrong or unjust. But they still hurt.

You may be wondering, though, why are we born with this spirit of rejection? Why are humans primed to have wounded hearts if God loves us so much? Why would He create us in this way?

To understand this process more fully, we need to turn our attention to the spiritual forces that act in the world, and act on us.

Spiritual Causes of Emotional Wounds

We have established the many ways – some big, some small – in which we become wounded in childhood. None of us can escape because we are children – we are vulnerable and even the "best" parents cannot control every aspect of a child's life. I learned this from experience. This begs the question – why does this happen?

Ladies and gentlemen, we have an enemy. That enemy's name is Satan, and he hates us because we love God. He is the epitome of evil and is the one responsible for directing the vast supernatural network of his followers. Some people call them demons.

If this news makes you uncomfortable, scoff in disbelief, or feel frightened because it appears spooky, turn right now to the Bible. Let us examine verses that demonstrate the reality of Satan, his spiritual followers, and his influence in our lives. Incidentally, in no way does this examination of Satan glorify or elevate his power. We glorify and worship only God the Father, the Creator of the heavens and the earth.

In conjunction with studying the character of God, it is also prudent to know the tactics and strategy of the forces that work in opposition to God. Some of these forces are social and natural. But the most influential of these forces is supernatural. Just as in wartime, military leaders study their opponents – who they are, what do they believe, why do they believe it, what is their objective, and what are their strategies and tactics – the same process needs to occur as we pursue deeper emotional healing and wholeness.

The supernatural realm is unequivocally real. I explicitly state this because believing in the supernatural is sometimes viewed as unsophisticated or believing in myths.

I am acutely aware that discussing the unseen realm can skirt easily into unbiblical ideas of the new age movement. As I mentioned in the introduction to this book, it is imperative that you know the Word of God for yourself. I detest being deceived. Having been deceived due to not confirming whether what I learned agreed with the Bible, I have become quite skeptical. I am not easily swayed.

Therefore, I understand, perhaps more than most, if you have some concern about the unseen world. Rather than shrink from the topic, I encourage you to start with what God has said to us in the Bible about angels, demons, and spirits. A full examination of the supernatural is beyond the scope of this book, but I would refer the interested Bible student to books by Dr. Chuck Missler and Dr. Michael Hieser.

Let us begin with the book of Job. The events in Job revolve around God allowing Satan to torment this righteous man. Numerous verses refer to Satan, but I will list two:

- One day the angels came to present themselves before the LORD, and Satan also came with them. The LORD said to Satan, "Where have you come from?" Satan answered the LORD, "From roaming throughout the earth, going back and forth on it" (1:6). (Notice that God has a back-and-forth conversation with Satan.)
- The LORD said to Satan, "Very well, then, everything he has is in your power, but on the man himself do not lay a finger" (2:12).

From this book, we learn that one reason God allows Satan to influence people in the natural realm is to teach us a lesson of some sort. For Job, it was to break his spirit of pride.

We learn more about Satan in the book of Ezekiel. For a complete reading, please see Ezekiel 28, which describes Satan's background. We learn that God created Satan (named Lucifer) as an angel:

> You *were* the anointed cherub who covers; I established you; You were on the holy mountain of God; You walked back and forth in the midst of fiery stones. You *were* perfect in your ways from the day you were created, Till iniquity was found in you." (28:14-15)

Not only did God create Lucifer as an angel, but Lucifer was also above other angels, presumably at the same status as Gabriel and Michael, the archangels. Satan was perfect in beauty (28:12) and adorned by precious stones in the garden of Eden (28:13). Clearly, God formed Lucifer to hold a high position in His kingdom, but Lucifer's pride caused God to expel him from Heaven: "Your heart was lifted up because of your beauty. You corrupted your wisdom for the sake of your splendor; I cast you to the ground, I laid you before kings, That they might gaze at you" (Ezek 28: 17).

In Isaiah we learn what Lucifer did to get expelled from heaven:

> For you have said in your heart: "I will ascend into heaven, I will exalt my throne above the start. I will also sit on the mount of the congregation On the farthest sides of the north. I will ascend above the heights of the clouds. I will be like the Most High."

Satan decided to elevate himself to be on the same throne as God. Pride, hubris, and blasphemy oozed from Lucifer. Therefore, God cast him out of heaven, along with a third of the angels (demons) (Rev 12:3-4).

Jesus Christ witnessed Satan's descent as he was being thrown to the earth, as recorded in Luke 10:18: "And He said to them, 'I was watching when Satan fell from heaven like lightning.'" You might note that Jesus speaks to, and about, Satan and demons throughout the Gospels.

Satan's stated purposes on the earth are important for us to know, as Paul reminds us in 2 Corinthians 2:11, "in order that no advantage be taken of us by Satan; for we are not ignorant of his schemes." He exists in direct opposition to God. His goal is always to exalt himself above God. Recall how he tempted Jesus after His 40 days in the wilderness – he tempted the Lord Jesus with food, with earthly possessions, and by appealing to possible issues of pride ("If you are the son of God throw Yourself down; for it is written, 'He will give his angels charge concerning you'" Matt 4:6).

Perhaps the most alarming verse showing the seriousness with which Satan does his job is found in 1 Peter 5:8-9: "Be sober, be vigilant; because your adversary the devil walks about like a roaring lion, seeking whom he may devour. Resist him, steadfast in the faith, knowing that the same sufferings are experienced by your brotherhood in the world."

I take some time to present this information to you so you can understand the reality of your adversary. He is not metaphoric, harmless, or simply a nuisance. In fact, he exists to kill, steal, and destroy (John 10:10). Our enemy is serious about his role. In fact, he is so serious that he targets us at our most vulnerable state of being – as a child.

Those hurts and wounds inflicted during your childhood have a source behind them. Satan is responsible for hurling lies, pain, and deception. When a child is being molested, the abuser is acting out his evil influences. An abuser is not a person who is merely disturbed. Evil is real. The enemy influences people. That abuser is allowing himself to function under the control of evil, whether he is conscious of it or not.

When children are abused, it is very common that the abuser says something like Anna's abuser – "You are worthless, you are dirty, no one can ever love you now because you are tainted." These statements, although being stated by a human being, in fact, originated from an evil source. The abuser is not simply being mean. He is acting out the evil impulses suggested to him when he was young, or during a critical developmental time period in his life that went awry.

Satan and his realm work by influencing people's thoughts. Just as Lucifer tempted Adam and Eve with a simple deceptive suggestion ("Did God really say..." Gen 3:1b), dark spirits make tempting suggestions that seem reasonable. I cannot pretend to understand how the unseen realm operates, but clearly, a portion of our minds picks up on spiritual chatter. We can know when God speaks to us through the Holy Spirit, so it should not be surprising that other spirits have ways of not only communicating with each other, but that humans can somehow tune into that chatter.

Clearly the demonic realm influences abusers. They have immoral urges that they believe are uncontrollable, so they act on them. They know they are wrong, which is why they threaten their victims to ensure they keep silent about the abuse.

In hurling the threatening statements at the victims, Satan's lies are passed on to a new generation. When a small child endures the pain and humiliation of being molested or beaten, they feel shame and embarrassment. Then the abuser says they also are dirty, unlovable, and worthless.

Guess what that child believes about him or herself as they grow up? How could they *not* believe the worst about themselves? At a vulnerable stage in life, someone violates them in unspeakable ways, and then when they have been physically beaten down and full of shame, their minds are unable to mount a defense against the heinous comments.

So they believe them to be true. Why would a child believe anything else about themselves? And in the secrecy that allows abuse to continue and thrive, the child replays in his mind those comments repeatedly. Eventually, those horrendous beliefs become second nature to the growing child. Young people lack the spiritual and cognitive capacity to discern truth from lies.

Since it *feels* true that they are dirty and worthless, given what happened to them, then it must *be* true. Whether the accusations come from a person or the child picks up on spiritual chatter, the source of all lies is Satan. He is a liar and the father of lies (John 8:44). Often, humans do the work for Satan. Other times, a demon influences a person directly. Even Christians can be influenced by demons.

(While there is a debate among Christians about whether a Christ follower can be possessed – the theory being that a Christian has the Holy Spirit inside him or her, and therefore no evil spirit can exist alongside the Holy Spirit – there is no debate that Christians can be influenced or even oppressed by evil entities. These differ from demonic possession. Please consult trusted sources for more perspectives on this issue.)

Regardless of how the lies are transmitted from person to person, and generation to generation, all lies come from demonic sources. From an emotional healing standpoint, the problem occurs when we choose to BELIEVE those lies about ourselves rather than what God says about who we are in Christ. This is the wound we seek to heal when we talk about inner healing or emotional healing.

So what exactly gets wounded that we need to heal in order to more fully live out God's will and purpose for our lives? Specifically, what needs healing? Where does the wound exist?

Chapter Seven: The Heart of the Matter

When Anna was molested by her family member as a child, not only was the experience itself devastating and painful, but her cousin's parting words to her changed her identity for decades. He told her she was now dirty and useless and that no one would want her, or love her, ever again.

In that one moment, the lies of the enemy pierced her heart and inflicted a wound that derailed her from God's purpose for her life. During traumatic events, our emotional and spiritual guards come down. This makes us highly vulnerable to other types of attacks, including those leveled at us from both spiritual and physical sources. In Anna's situation, she not only felt embarrassment and hurt from the molestation, but additionally, she was now burdened by the belief that she was forever unlovable and unwanted. The nasty lies her abuser spat at her functioned as curses.

Because Anna was still in a state of shock over the experience, her vulnerability was extensive. Again, this happens in most traumatic situations when our guards come down. It means that our ability to properly discern the truth is deactivated. Also, these types of situations tend to happen to children – talk about the height of evil! Satan is so serious about defeating children of God that he unleashes his attacks at our most vulnerable time: when we are children and during a violation of some kind. Satan may not be creative, but he is strategic. He knows what happens to us during challenging moments and he takes advantage.

In Anna's mind, because the abuse made her feel dirty, uncomfortable, and powerless when her family member sneered his lies at her, they felt true. These ideas of her being permanently unlovable seemed consistent with what she experienced. So why would she not believe them? At her moment of victimization and powerlessness, her vulnerability could not have been higher. This is exactly when the lies from the enemy become most effective. They seem to confirm what she started to think about herself. Plus, the message came from someone older who had just exerted power and force over her (albeit illegitimate, of course). Therefore, the message he spat out at Anna carried even more credibility.

This is the moment a wound was inflicted. But where was this wound located?

God tells us in Proverbs 4:23 to "keep your heart with all diligence." The reason we are to do so is because of the next part of the same verse: "For out of it spring the issues of life."

Other versions of the Bible translate this verse as follows: "Above all else, guard your heart, for everything you do flows from it" (NIV). Let us take some time to dissect this powerful teaching verse.

Think of the issues of your life. What do you struggle with? What mountains do you find yourself repeatedly going around, wishing they would go away or resolve? What relationship hurts do you carry with you? Do you have trouble trusting people? Do you find yourself constantly feeling disappointed in, or betrayed by, people in your life? Do you grapple with depression, anxiety, relationship problems, constant resentment, jealousy, or discouragement?

Remember where God says these issues stem from – your heart. Remind yourself what He tells you to do *above all else*: to guard (or keep) your heart. It is when our hearts are unguarded that they become vulnerable to injury, wounding, or hurts. We know this because of the issues of our lives. They come from our hearts, and because our issues are clearly not from God (God will never disappoint you or make you feel depressed, dejected, anxious, or discouraged), we know that our hearts must somehow be wrong or misguided.

How, exactly, can a heart be misguided? To understand how this works, we need to delve into more of God's Word and His statements about the purpose of our hearts. Then you will more clearly see how the wounding we experience is on our hearts.

In the following verses, I will emphasize the portions that refer to the heart. You should notice a trend emerge about the role of our hearts.

> For the *hearts of this people have grown dull.* Their ears are hard of hearing, And their eyes they have closed, Lest they should see with their eyes and hear with their ears, *Lest they should understand with their hearts and turn, So that I should heal them.* (Matt 13:15)

> If you confess with your mouth the Lord Jesus and *believe in your heart* that God has raised Him from the dead, you will be saved. *For with the heart one believes unto righteousness,* and with the mouth confession is made unto salvation. (Rom 10:9-10)

> But God be thanked that though you were slaves of sin, yet *you obeyed from the heart* that form of doctrine to which you were delivered. (Rom 6:17)

> [Gentiles] show the work of *the law written in their hearts....* (Rom 2:15a)

> For where your treasure is, *there your heart will be also.* (Luke 12:34)

> And I, indeed I, have appointed with him Aholiab the son of Ahisamach, of the tribe of Dan; and *I have put wisdom in the hearts of all the gifted artisans,* that they may make all that I have commanded you. (Exod 31:6)

> Then Moses called Bezalel and Aholiab, and every gifted artisan *in whose heart the LORD had put wisdom, everyone whose heart was stirred,* to come and do the work. (Exod 36:2)

> You shall *love the LORD your God with all your heart,* and all your soul, and with all your strength. (Deut 6:5)

Only take heed to yourself, and diligently keep yourself, lest you forget the things your eyes have seen, and *lest they depart from your heart* all the days of your life. (Deut 4:9a)

For the LORD does not see as a man sees; for man looks at the outward appearance, but *the LORD looks at the heart.* (1 Sam 16:7b)

Your word I have hidden in my heart, That I might not sin against You. (Ps 119:11)

But this is the covenant that I will make with the house of Israel after those days, says the LORD; I will put My law in their minds, and *write it on their hearts.* (Jer 31:33)

In the preceding verses, God has told us quite a bit about why we need to guard our hearts. To summarize:
- We understand things in our hearts (Matt 13:15).
- We believe things in our hearts (Rom 10:6-10).
- Our obedience originates in our hearts (Rom 6:17).
- We love with our hearts (Deut 6:5).
- It is the place the Lord looks (1 Sam 16).
- It is located at the place of our treasure (Luke 12:34).
- It is where God places wisdom (Exod 31:6 and 36:2).
- It is where our memory resides (Deut 4:9).
- It is the place where God's Word resides (Ps 119:11).
- It is where God writes His law and His will (Jer 31:33 and Rom 2:15).

When God wants us to understand something, not simply have an intellectual knowledge of His Word that we can recite from memory, He puts His knowledge on our hearts. Your heart is the central holding place of the things you believe. We *know* things in our brains, but we *believe* things in our hearts. The intentions of our actions and motivations lie in our hearts. We "know" facts, data, and information in our minds. But in our hearts reside the nucleus of our motivations and drive.

You can prove this to yourself right now by reciting any verse of Scripture that you like and then asking yourself if you 100%

believe that Scripture to be true for YOU. Let me give you some examples:

> Do you believe in your heart that, in Christ, you are *assured* of success (Prov 16:3)?
>
> Do you believe in your heart that you are beautiful and a masterpiece (Song 4:7; Eph 2:10)?
>
> Do you believe you are bold and confident (Eph 3:12)?
>
> Are you confident that He will never leave you and that He has never left you (Heb 13:5-6)?
>
> Do you believe in your heart that you have a spirit of power, love, and discipline, and not of fear (2 Tim 1:7)?
>
> Do you believe wholeheartedly that you are inseparable from His love and that there is nothing you can do to keep God from loving you (Rom 8:35)?
>
> Do you really trust in the Lord with all of your heart, and lean not on your own understanding (Pro 3:5)?
>
> Do you believe in your heart that you are part of the royal priesthood and are a prince or princess as a child of the King (1 Pet 2:9)?
>
> Do you fully believe in your heart that you are qualified to share Christ's inheritance (Rom 8:17; Col 1:12)?
>
> Do you believe, in the deepest parts of your heart, that you are victorious (1 Cor 15:57)?
>
> Do you believe, with 100% certainty of your whole being, that God loves you with an everlasting love (Jer 31:3)?

As you read these truths from God – truths about you, your identity, your future, and your present moment – was any part of you wondering if they were really *true about you?*

At any moment, did you think, "Yes, I believe this....or actually, *I want to believe it, but I don't think it's true for me.*"

Christians have a major gap problem. We have memorized Scripture and can recite it, oftentimes chapter and verse. But we do not believe the Scriptures apply to us. *We only HOPE the Scripture is true for us;* we do not actually believe it to be factual for us. We are great at praying these things over other people. And in our tough moments, we confess these Scriptures over ourselves.

But how many times do you find yourself reciting Scripture with a portion of you wondering if it is really true? Does even one percent of you have doubt? I urge you to be honest with yourself.....and with God. Of course, God knows where your doubts reside even if you fail to acknowledge them. Admitting them to yourself is the first step to allowing God to lovingly correct your doubts.

The point here is that most of us do not really grasp the truth of God's Word about us and the world around us. We know it intellectually, but in our hearts, we believe the opposite.

This is what happened with Anna. She knew that God loved her – at least in her mind. But in her heart, she *really* believed she was unlovable. How can a person believe two contradictory concepts? It is not possible. It means we have memorized something in our brains, but what we really believe resides in our hearts.

If I told you that two plus two equals five, and that you could not withdraw money from your bank account unless you were able to recite this mathematical equation, you would certainly have the capacity to recite it. You would go to the bank, dutifully say that two plus two equals five, get your money, and be on your merry way.

However, deep down in your heart, you would believe something very different. You would know, for a fact, that two plus two equals four. You would know this because of your own personal experience. The events in your life have shown you, repeatedly, that two plus two equals four. Therefore, you could, if you absolutely had to, recite two plus two equals five.....but never fully believe it in your heart.

The same process applies to everything, especially our identity. God says one thing about us, but oftentimes our personal history has strongly proven something else. Anna knew in her mind that God loves her. But at that pivotal moment back when she was a little girl, she learned something about herself that is the opposite of what God says, but it "feels" very true. Specifically, Anna believed she was unlovable. She could confess with her mouth that God loves her, and she wanted desperately for those words to be true. Yet she failed to believe them. She would try to convince herself that God loves her by denying and avoiding her creeping thoughts like, "No one can love me because of what happened. I'm never good enough, I am dirty and unworthy and unimportant." When those thoughts crept in, Anna would do the "right thing" by reciting Scriptures over and over.

While confessing the truth of God's Word over your life is so important, it may also be true that you are repeating those Scriptures as a way of convincing yourself out of your false beliefs. In some instances, this does work. Over time, reciting the truth of the Word of God does sink down into your heart, change the false beliefs you had, and shift you into alignment with what God says about you.

But in working with people over the years, I have found that there are some issues that do not relent in this way. Sometimes the wound on our hearts is so deep, so profound, and such a stronghold that no amount of logic or reciting Bible verses can overcome those lies.

In these cases, only a supernatural encounter with God Almighty Himself can fix the problem. A word from Him, a specific, intimate, and powerful word directly from God carries the gravity of veritas, a weight of objective truth that is undeniable.

Your heart has been the target of the enemy perhaps even before you were born. Remember, you have a purpose inside God's kingdom. If you operate primarily within your wounded heart, you will be hindered in your journey to live out His purpose for you. Just as a broken leg dramatically reduces your ability to move around, in the same way, your wounded heart makes it extremely challenging to move forward the path set before you.

This happens because the wounds on your heart cause you to believe wrong things about yourself. You might believe, for instance, that, "I am dirty, I am unlovable, I am invisible, I am unimportant, I don't deserve to live, I have no purpose, my voice doesn't matter, I don't matter." These are examples of the beliefs I have heard my clients and conference and retreat attendees admit to having.

How can you confidently pursue a leadership position in your community when you believe in your heart that you are unimportant? How can you hope to have a healthy marriage if you believe you cannot trust people....or God? How can you build your business if you believe you are invisible and unworthy of being taken seriously? How can you have healthy and strong relationships with your children and other family members if you believe you are unlovable? How can forge lasting and effective relationships in your workplace, community groups, or family if you believe you are unimportant?

You can see why your heart is the target of the enemy. Making sure you believe things in direct opposition to God's truth about who you are keeps you constrained, nervous to move forward, and scared to take even the safest risks for growth. If you spend most of your time expecting people to let you down and disappoint you because you believe in your heart that no one can be trusted, how can you nurture a loving and deep marriage? How can you teach your children about being properly vulnerable in the context of a loving, trusting relationship when you cannot do it yourself?

A broken, wounded, and beaten-up heart keeps you bound and restricted far more than any physical malady ever could. What you believe in your heart becomes the issues you grapple with. Your heart tells your brain what to do, or not do, based on what you believe. Your brain listens to your heart because your heart holds your understanding of yourself and the world around you.

When you find you believe in your heart something contrary to the Word of God, like most of us do, it is time to acknowledge your broken heart to the One who can and will heal it.

But how do the heart and the brain communicate? How do beliefs drive feelings, behavior, and outcome? This is where psychology can step in and bring some clarity.

The Establishment of Core Beliefs and the Limitations of Psychology

We have lots of beliefs and thoughts about everything in our world. These beliefs are formed and shaped by our experiences, our environment, the people around us, our family situation, the books we read (or do not read!), the internet sites we use, and the news sources we access.

Most beliefs are surface-level thoughts. These are the thoughts we have that help us function throughout the day – what we believe about our ability to drive to a new location, manage our daily workload, why we speak to whom we speak, what we say to them, and even what we choose to wear. The list is endless.

But when it comes to emotional pain, we need to talk about a specific type of belief. Psychologists call this group of beliefs our "core beliefs." These refer to specific, fundamental, and very basic beliefs we have about ourselves at the most foundational level. These are the beliefs we hold at the very center of our being.

These beliefs can be positive, neutral, or negative. But they tend to exist unconsciously and we operate out of them automatically. They are formed primarily (but not exclusively) during childhood. Certainly, our parents play a large role in the development of those beliefs. As you have seen through Anna's story, beliefs also develop as a result of life experiences. Everything you have encountered since the day you were born has imprinted itself in some way in your brain.

From the psychotherapy approach called Cognitive-Behavioral therapy, we can put some structure to understand how all of this "stuff" works together and how we need to change (or allow God to change) our beliefs in order to have a breakthrough in our emotions and behaviors. Over the past few decades, psychological research has identified a specific pathway that links our behaviors to our emotions and our beliefs. Here is how they all fit together.

You have an event or circumstance happen in your life, and they vary in significance. Sometimes the event is minor, and sometimes it is major. But to understand the process, I suggest focusing on a relatively minor one to help illustrate the basic concept. The example I like to use is one that most of us can relate to – driving on a very busy highway.

Imagine yourself driving on a highway that has a reputation for crazy or erratic driving. I like to suggest the Washington, DC beltway, because of my own personal experiences on it, but you can think of whatever roadway fits this description! Picture yourself driving on this road, minding your own business, when suddenly a car races up beside you and cuts right in front of you. The driver's sudden and quick movements mean you have to put your brakes on in order to avoid a collision.

In this circumstance, consider the thoughts that might go through your mind at the exact moment this happens. For most people, the thoughts probably resemble, "That so-and-so, who does he think he is! He almost killed me! What a jerk/lunatic/idiot." Some of you may have a more colorful language of choice in these instances. If so, you are not alone!

Then think about what happens next. After this driver is now in front of you, and you repeat to yourself what a jerk he is, think about how you are feeling. What emotion rises up? Are you angry? Irritated? Enraged? Ticked off? Scared? These emotional responses certainly make sense in this scenario.

Now consider what might happen next, with these unpleasant emotions running through your body. You might squeeze the steering wheel harder. Or you might grumble out loud, or even swear at the driver. Some people might make a hand gesture to convey their anger toward that driver. Other people might attempt to retaliate by tailgating the driver or trying to pass them so that driver "doesn't get away with it." In fact, the entire concept of road rage stems from this exact situation. Some people have such a short fuse that someone driving in this way triggers an escalation into an intense, possibly even dangerous condition.

Most people do not end up in rage, of course. But most of us do have a lot of irritation, and we might find that we carry that irritation with us long after the event happens. That driver is practically out of sight five minutes later, but we still rehash in our minds how stupid and jerk-like that driver was.

Now, let us rewind our imaginations and reconsider this situation from a different perspective. Again, imagine yourself driving along that busy highway. The man comes racing up beside you, and he cuts right in front of you, causing you to apply your breaks. This time, instead of saying to yourself, "What a jerk!" you say to yourself, "I wonder if that man's wife is in labor?" Or, "I wonder if his child is in the hospital and he needs to get there quickly?"

Consider how this thought process might cause a shift in how you feel and your emotional response to the situation. Thinking that he is driving erratically because of a reason that would likely have us driving in that same fashion takes the edge off our anger and irritation.

You may still have some concern and mild frustration because, in fact, his driving is dangerous. However, because we remove the judgmental condemnation of the driver from our minds, it feels less personal. It ratchets down our emotional reaction considerably. From this standpoint, we can even extend mercy toward that driver, because the truth is that we have no idea why he drove in that manner.

If every day, you see the same driver operating his vehicle in the same way, then you have evidence that yes, he may be selfish and highly inconsiderate. But in the absence of proof, why choose to assume a reason for his driving that only serves to make you needlessly angry? You give away your joy without any objective reason for it to be taken from you.

This example shows you how we operate emotionally and gives you a solution for changing your emotional reactions psychologically. We encounter an event in our lives. We have a thought or belief about that event. The thought or belief causes an emotional response, and this often leads to some behavior. The process looks like this:

> Event/Situation -→ Thought/Belief →
> Emotional Response → Behavior

Following this template, in our first driving example the structure looks like this:

> Car cuts in front → He's a jerk → Anger or intense irritation → clenching steering wheel, retaliation

In our second driving example, the structure looks like this (and please pay attention to the only thing that changed):

> Car cuts in front → His wife or child is in the hospital → Mildly concerned → Extend mercy, and go along as you were before

Notice the element that changes. The situation itself is the same in both scenarios, but the outcomes could not be more different. And it all centers on the thought or belief that runs through our minds in response to the event. When we change our thoughts and beliefs, we can directly change our emotions. When we change our emotions, our behavior changes as well.

Also, it is important to understand that there exist "levels" of beliefs and thoughts. We can have beliefs about issues that are relatively minor, or even completely unimportant. For instance, I have a deeply held belief that making left turns while driving puts me at unnecessary risk. When I was 18 years old, I had an accident that I caused while turning left at a stop sign. No one was hurt, but it felt scary. Since then, I avoid left-hand turns at stop signs as much as possible. In no way does this interfere with my life, or cause problems (other than my husband not completely understanding my avoidance of this situation – and in fact, it provides an opportunity for some lighthearted, but loving, teasing when I am driving!). I may know intellectually that I can safely make left turns, and in fact, have successfully made left turns probably hundreds of times since my accident. But that one time in which my turn resulted in an accident fused a certain belief in my heart.

While my aversion to left-hand turns is strong, it is not important. It is not something I pursue healing for because it does not cause any kind of problem. But not all beliefs and thoughts fall into this same category.

In many cases, our beliefs grow deeper into our hearts and contribute a great deal to our identity. They become a major shaper of our identity, what we are capable of, and what kind of future we can have. These deeper, more meaningful, and impactful beliefs psychologists refer to as "core beliefs." These core beliefs are the ones that typically stem from early childhood and are the ones Satan targets.

These beliefs drive the most important decisions we make on a daily basis. Believing that people intentionally drive like jerks does not impact our lives (unless you have road rage). But believing you are unlovable, unworthy, unimportant, condemned, shameful, dirty, or invisible has a direct, and negative, impact on the decisions you make daily about the most important issues in your life.

These core beliefs are the ones that get warped. Not only psychologists target these beliefs, but God wants His input on them as well. You can see how powerful it is to understand how our beliefs directly affect our emotions and behavior. As a psychologist, I would use this type of therapy for most issues that my clients and patients experienced. Even in my coaching practice, I use this model of understanding behavior as a way of helping my leadership clients grow and change.

This therapeutic modality has decades of research and clinical support showing how effectively it helps people alleviate depressive and anxiety-related symptoms. In fact, most therapists incorporate this model in some way during their work with clients and patients.

However, I encountered a problem, which caused me to question how "good" of a therapist I was. When I first started working with a client, I would explain the concept of Cognitive-Behavioral therapy. In fact, teaching clients the rationale behind the therapy empowers them to be able to apply the strategies across many areas of their lives. I would usually use the same driving example I used above, and I would explain the relationship between life events, thoughts, feelings, and behaviors using a chart.

Every so often, a client would come in and simply not "buy into" the driving example. Perhaps in 25% of my cases, the client would say something like, "No way, that guy is just a jerk, pure and simple." In other words, these clients would not see any way that this driver's intentions could be situational and excusable. While these clients understood the basic theory of the therapy technique, for the most part, they did not seem to improve as much as other clients who did recognize alternative reasons for driving in that manner.

When I first started encountering this situation, I was a relatively young therapist. Therefore, I started wondering, "What is wrong with me that I cannot get through to this person?" I believed it was my own inadequacies that prevented the client from fully understanding the process. Over the years, I found myself frustrated that I could not "get through to" these people. If only I were a better therapist, I could convey this more effectively, and help them improve their moods.

Yet this gap still existed for a certain percentage of people. In fact, some of you reading the driving example will likely have had the same reaction when you read it. "Oh, I know for a fact that guy is a jerk, and he's just driving like that out of arrogance and because he doesn't care about other people." (By the way, it is completely fine if you had that thought! My whole point in explaining this is to acknowledge that not everyone will automatically agree with the example.)

Why did some people react in this way? What could explain why intelligent, thoughtful people refused to believe that someone driving erratically on the highway might have a perfectly good reason to drive in that manner? What was I missing?

In my coaching practice, I experienced far less of this situation. Yet I could not stop wondering why this happened. Part of it was my tendency toward perfectionism. These people who did not agree with my driving example were proof that "I am not good enough, and I cannot be an effective therapist."

But God showed me the reason this happens, and it highlights a deficiency in secular mental health care. During my fast in which God healed me, He also is the One who revealed the power of personal experience to "teach" us things about ourselves and the world, some of which are accurate and some of which are downright lies.

For the people who did not want to believe an alternative explanation for the driver's behavior, it was because they had personal experience that "proved" they were right. Most likely they personally witnessed drivers who did behave selfishly and without regard for others.

When our personal experiences teach us something, very little logic, rational thought, or convincing can make us change our minds. We might even realize that it doesn't make sense for us to believe something false. But that belief feels right, it feels comfortable, and it feels true. Even when confronted with Scriptures that contradict our long-held beliefs, we resist relenting to God's truth.

When God's truth does not mesh with our personal experience, and we seem stuck in our ability to override and replace our experience with God's Word, we require a more powerful intervention. When we know God's Word in our minds, yet believe something contradictory in our hearts, there is a gap. That gap between our minds and our hearts can seem enormous, and like it can never be closed.

This is where Christians often find themselves defeated. You might feel defeated in certain areas too. That space between the place where God's truth lives in your mind but seems distant and unattainable to your heart has an even more discouraging quality to it. That gap between knowing Scripture and believing Scripture as true for you appears to "confirm" that God's hand is not available to you. You may think, "I have spent years studying God's Word, memorizing Scripture, reciting it every day, claiming it for myself. Yet breakthrough has not come – I still struggle in major ways."

You are not the only person in this situation. It is not because you have not tried hard enough, or that you lack enough faith. It is not because God has abandoned you, or that only some parts of God's Word apply to you, and not all of it. God is faithful to His Word, and His Word will not return void (Isa 55:11). He promises healing for you, so He will provide it for you.

Our role in allowing Him to close this gap is to put ourselves in the proper position to receive His healing. This means being still. It means allowing God to be God, and for us to humble ourselves in acknowledging His power to lovingly correct our wrong beliefs.

Only He can close this gap. Once we realize our own inability to override our personal experiences that we mistakenly took as "truth," we can hold those misguided beliefs up to Him. He will tell us His truth, which is the truth. His intimate, direct, and loving communication to us will immediately bind up the wounds inflicted by years of believing a lie. Because God makes all things new again (Rev 21:5), once our hearts are healed, they are new. It means that, going forward, the healed heart will function as if it had never been wounded! Praise God!

It is time to allow God to heal your heart. Psychotherapy has its limitations, as you can see. Therefore, only a direct touch from God can close some of the gaps in your life.

Now that you understand why you want to allow God to heal the false core beliefs that act as wounds to your heart, you may wonder why it is so hard for God to get through to us. Why can't we just pray for God to heal us and He does it immediately? What is the hold-up?

One again, we will look to psychology to help you understand how we all get in our own way when it comes to healing. In fact, we tend to keep God at a distance from us, unconsciously. Let's learn how this happens so we can find a solution!

Trying to Fix the Problem on Our Own – Keeping God at a Distance

Why is it so hard? God knows the wounds on our hearts, He knows exactly what happened when they were inflicted, and He knows exactly what we need for our healing? So – *why doesn't He DO SOMETHING?*

I wish I had a satisfying answer to this question. But the reality is that our wounds happen, and they remain unhealed because we live in a fallen world that seeks, at every turn, to exalt people over the sovereignty of God. You have learned that your heart is the target of an enemy whose singular focus is to oppose everything related to God. Therefore, Satan and his followers wound us at the points of our greatest vulnerability. Our vulnerable nature exists because of our human nature of self-centeredness. This means that normal, daily experiences create wounds and hurts that create emotional pain.

When we experience pain, it is so uncomfortable and unpleasant that we immediately search for ways to make that pain go away. Some people react this way to physical pain. They reach for the pain medicine the moment a headache starts. Other people can tolerate physical pain differently and may try to tough it out.

But when it comes to emotional pain, most people react quickly to make the pain disappear. We experience anxiety, rejection, shame, guilt, discouragement, defeat, or stress, and rather than using those emotions productively, we instead work immediately to squash them or avoid them altogether.

There are two categories of ways we seek to deal with emotional pain on our own. Psychologists refer to these categories as defense mechanisms and coping mechanisms (or sometimes the word "strategies" is used). Defense mechanisms refer to the things we do in our minds in order to defend ourselves from hurt and pain. These are the inner psychological processes we use subconsciously and automatically. I often refer to them as "mental gymnastics." On the other hand, when we seek to actively avoid or run away from the pain, we employ various coping mechanisms, and this term refers to the behaviors we engage in. I will explain the two categories so you can understand how you use them, the objectives each are trying to achieve, and how knowing this can help you allow more of God into your heart to heal it.

Defense Mechanisms – Trying to Prevent More Pain by Relying on Our Defense

You and your husband come home after long days at work. As you walk into the house, you realize you forgot to pick up something for dinner, although you had promised your husband that you would do it. Unfortunately, this is the sixth time this month you promised him you would arrange for dinner and you did not. The guilt starts to creep up in your mind because you know your husband will get angry and feel like you do not care about him.

But instead of allowing that uncomfortable and unpleasant guilt to creep in any further, you engage your "mental gymnastics" so you can avoid dealing with the fact you did not follow through on something. Your failure to follow through on the promise to your husband triggers your memory of your father telling you how disappointed he was in you. That wound from childhood runs deep and carries so much pain that you seek to avoid reminders of that pain at all costs. That triggered wound makes you recall a core belief about yourself: I am a loser and totally incompetent.

If you, at that moment, connected with that false belief of your total worthlessness, you would experience debilitating emotional pain. You would likely start crying and become unable to function for the rest of the evening. Rather than experience this, our minds work to help us avoid those painful memories and beliefs. These mental gymnastics also serve the purpose of attempting to deflect the anger your husband would legitimately have toward you onto something else.

To achieve all this, you might say something like, "You always forget to remind me, and you know how crazy my schedule is! If you really want me to bring home dinner, you would at least text me a reminder."

You walk away thinking, "See, it's his problem, not mine, so I do not have to apologize or correct myself." You walk with a sense of righteous indignation toward your husband, which protects your heart from emotional pain.

But the other impact your mental gymnastics has is to create conflict with your husband, widening the differences between the two of you and stoking the fire of discord and unhappiness in your marriage. When you believe it is "all his fault," you also start to believe, "He cannot take care of me, he does not care about me, he is only thinking about himself and his selfish needs."

Psychologists refer to this as "projection." As one of the more common defense mechanisms, projection means we take our own feelings or motivations and accuse another person of those feelings or motivations. We project our "stuff" onto someone else, and we view that other person as having the exact problem we have. Yet we fail to recognize it in ourselves.

In the example above, the wife places her own insecurities about incompetence and places them on her husband. Her true fear is that it is she who cannot take care of herself and her family, and by blaming her husband, she, in fact, is the one who is selfish and uncaring.

Projection is extremely common, and we all do it to some extent. The next time you feel compelled to accuse someone or blame someone of something, take a moment to ask yourself if you feel the same way you are accusing the other person of feeling. Or do you accuse another of doing the thing you fear you do, but do not want to admit? This is quite humbling, yet Jesus Himself told us to examine the plank in your own eye before pointing out the speck in someone else's (Matt 7:3-5). Many defense mechanisms cause us to behave hypocritically.

Another type of defense mechanism is known as denial. When we deny something, we refuse to accept a reality or a fact. The most common example is when we hear about the untimely death of someone we love, our initial reaction is, "NO! I cannot believe it! It cannot be true." We react in this manner because we want to avoid the intense pain of acknowledging a tragic situation. Rather than allow the feeling of that pain, we push away the reality of the situation.

Denial lies at the heart of many horrendous issues. For instance, people battling an addiction to drugs, alcohol, pornography, or any other substance rely heavily on denial. A person struggling with alcohol will claim he has no problem because he functions at work and still brings home a paycheck. A drug addict will insist that she can control her use of the drug and that her use is not as bad as everyone thinks it is. A person addicted to pornography will tell you that it harms no one and is no big deal. People in active addictions tell themselves, and others, that "this is ok," and no one notices. Meanwhile, they fail to acknowledge the family members who plead with them to quit, or the boss who keeps telling them that they really need to improve their performance or they risk losing their job.

Denial also allows abuse, particularly sexual abuse, to continue. I cannot tell you how often I have heard about households in which the father abused a daughter and that grown daughter insists her mother must have known about it. It is probably very true that the mother should have been aware. But because the mother herself likely experienced similar abuse, she wanted to avoid re-experiencing her own pain. The mother achieved this goal by failing to recognize and then protect her daughter.

In these cases, if the parent does become consciously aware of the child's victimhood, it would not only trigger the adult parent's own pain, but it would force her or him to drastic action. Acknowledging abuse in a household means the parent has to make one of two life-changing choices: either outwardly acknowledge and then deal with the consequences of accusing the spouse or remain in denial and sacrifice the child for the sake of not disturbing the marriage and family situation.

Denial also occurs frequently when a spouse is cheating on the other spouse. A wife may have an inkling that her husband is stepping out on her. But if she allows that doubt to surface, she faces extremely painful situations. Either she chooses to leave her husband (and the turmoil and upheaval associated with that decision) or she chooses to stay and work on the marriage, which involves dredging up her own issues along with the hard work of restoring a broken relationship. In addition, sometimes a person feels very self-conscious about choosing to remain with a spouse who was unfaithful. The person may worry that others view her as weak or a doormat if she stays with him.

In so many cases, it becomes easier to remain in denial. This is extremely sad and, of course, devastating for others involved. Yet it happens every day, in all sorts of situations. All defense mechanisms involve our minds distorting reality. I frequently refer to them as "mental gymnastics" because of the gyrations we go through to make life situations seem okay and tolerable, when, in fact, they are far from okay and tolerable. Therefore, you probably have already realized that defense mechanisms are not godly. They are anything but godly, since they involve only our own minds to change, reinterpret, or alter our perceptions of reality. In our humanness, we employ these automatic strategies to avoid the intense anxiety, angst, or pain that rises up in trigger situations. And we all engage in at least one of these mechanisms.

Another common psychological defense mechanism is called displacement. Imagine being at work and your boss puts extra pressure on you to be more productive, even though you already feel maxed out with your time and energy. Your boss might even subtly make it known to you that your job might be in jeopardy if your performance does not increase. Naturally, you will have some emotional reactions to your boss and the added pressure she is placing on you. You might feel stressed, incapable of meeting the demand, angry at your boss for putting you in this situation, and perhaps defeated. Despite the intensity of all these emotions, you simply cannot unload them all on your boss.

When you arrive home, with all this stuff churning under the surface in your mind, your son comes up to you and shows you a pile of paperwork you have to sign for school, and it is due the next day, including the teacher needing you to chaperone a field trip next week. What happens? You scream at him and transfer all the frustration and hurt caused by your workplace situation onto your son. And it is not pretty.

You are not genuinely angry with your son, and in fact, you normally would love to chat with him about his upcoming field trip as you sign all the papers. But your mind is on overload and your emotions wound so tightly that a relatively insignificant thing unleashes the force of your pushed-down emotions in the blink of an eye.

Transferring negative emotions toward one thing onto another target is displacement. We displace our anger, worry, and resentment onto something completely unrelated and away from the true source of our pain. I believe we all can reflect on a time or two when we have done this. Perhaps when you have caught yourself doing this, you may have gone back to apologize to the unintended target of your emotional stuff. I know I certainly have!

Yet another defense mechanism I want to mention is called reaction formation. It is a weird name and can seem difficult to grasp at first, but it is very common. This happens when we have an emotional reaction, but that emotion is socially unacceptable for whatever reason. Instead of expressing the real emotion we feel, we express the exact opposite of what we feel. We go overboard in expressing the opposite emotion of what we actually experience. In William Shakespeare's *Hamlet,* the famous line, "The lady doth protest too much," nicely demonstrates reaction formation. This line has become a figure of speech when we believe someone's emphatic stance on something is probably masking their true, and opposite, opinion about the topic.

When we "kill someone with kindness," we might be displaying a reaction formation response. This phrase implies that we seriously disagree or dislike someone, but instead of acting out our displeasure, we direct our energies to very kind behaviors. This specific instance could be Christ-like, but only when we acknowledge and are honest about our true feelings. Any time we seek to avoid or distort our true feelings and the reality of a situation, we are not acting within God's will, although outwardly it may look as though we are. God wants us to be honest so He can then prompt us to forgive someone if needed or to pursue reconciliation or restoration in relationships.

While reaction formation can be tough to understand if you have never heard of it, I include it in the book because I commonly encounter it in my healing ministry. When I work with someone to take their faulty beliefs and lies to God, and to ask Him to speak to the person directly and intimately, sometimes the person says, "Oh, I have such a feeling of peace," or, "Wow, I feel so excited and elated!"

It happens automatically, and unconsciously. Some people have their defenses kick in because they mistakenly believe that hearing from God will be unpleasant or scary. To guard against this potential "emotional injury," their unconscious mind creates an intense emotion that feels good and satisfying. I know it has happened when I ask the person, "Did God say anything to you?" and the response is along the lines of, "I feel such a sense of peace/elation/joy!" You might note that the person does not acknowledge a direct message from God, but only a shift in their emotional state.

This might be difficult to wrap your head around, but "knowing" something is entirely different from "feeling" something. When God speaks to a person, He brings the authority and truth of the Creator of the universe to His statements. When you hear from God, you will know it. You will not "feel" it. You will KNOW it, just like you know that two plus two equals four. You do not "feel" that two plus two equals four. You simply know it. You will know God's voice and the truth it carries. Most people cry upon hearing God's voice, not out of emotion, but rather out of release and relief. If you notice a strong emotional reaction that seems to be the opposite of what you normally experience when you think about your troubling self-thoughts, consider that you did not yet hear from God. This happens so automatically and "feels" so positive that it seems like something major should have happened. Likely, though, your defenses rose up to block your heart from God's words to you. If this is the case, keep pressing in, and keep praying to ask God to reveal your defensive moves and help you to break them down.

I will add here that, in order to properly understand and evaluate our behavior and thoughts, we must become still. To examine ourselves requires introspection and willingness to admit when we are wrong or misguided. This challenges not only our anxieties but also our pride. No one likes to admit when we are wrong. But when we allow subconscious, automatic reactions to rule our relationships, our wounds end up damaging other people. When our wounds become another person's problem, it is important to pull back the pride, take a time-out, and be honest with ourselves about our motivations.

Being still helps make this happen. We must allow that stillness. We must be prepared for feeling emotions we do not like. Remember, we develop these defenses as ways of avoiding unpleasant feelings. Making a priority of your personal healing involves an investigation of how we treat other people, which eventually leads us to our own pain.

You have heard the expression, "Hurting people hurt others." This is so true. In fact, we will examine in chapter eight why this happens. But indeed, our wounds end up bleeding onto other people. This creates conflict, more hurt feelings, and alienation from the ones who love us the most. Stillness will bring all of this to the surface. Do not be afraid of this process. Embrace it, because in stillness, you will find God, and He will be with you during your healing journey. It is also true that "Transformed people transform others." Your healing can lead others to their healing opportunities.

One last defense mechanism I want to explore is the one I use the most, and my guess is that you do too. It is our "go-to" method of trying to cope with unpleasant situations and emotions. It is called intellectualization, or rationalization.

Intellectualization occurs when we automatically try to explain away an emotion or to create distance from the emotion by explaining it away. This can neutralize anxiety, disappointment, or dejection by finding a "rational" reason or cause for the situation. We come up with logical reasons for a situation, so we avoid dealing with how much pain that situation causes.

On September 11, 2001, I was at work at the pain center where I was the staff psychologist. Everyone who came into the office – staff and patients alike – were in a state of shock at the events that were unfolding. Over the course of about two hours, as we watched the first tower collapse, we felt such deep devastation at how many thousands of people were likely being killed right before our eyes. One of the office staff said, "Well, this might kill 5,000 people, but so many more people are killed each year in drunk driving accidents."

While I do not know how many people are killed each year by drunk drivers, the exact number was irrelevant to what was going on that day. But the series of catastrophic events was so intense that this person tried to find a way to distance herself from the sadness. She did this by intellectualizing the situation. In comparing the terror attacks to drunk driving, she was seeking to make the impact of September 11 less impactful in her mind.

The moment the comment escaped her lips, I knew what she was doing and why she was doing it. There was no reason to argue or confront her, but it created an uncomfortable atmosphere in the room where we watched the live feed from New York City. A few people in the room nodded in agreement with her comment because it probably was true. But it clearly felt "off" and certainly did not seem like it was a reasonable comparison.

The reason it felt "off" is that it was a defense mechanism kicking in, seeking to help this person avoid dealing with the enormity of what was occurring. It would be tough to engage denial – we were watching it on live television. And reaction formation would have meant she would have probably laughed. But intellectualizing the events was almost too easy, and indeed I heard many people say similar things over the days that immediately followed the attacks.

While I cannot recall deploying intellectualization after the terror attacks, I tended to do it a lot in other ways. Incidentally, this was one of the things God healed me of! But before my healing, I would rationalize why other people's needs are more important than my own. In fact, that is why I avoided my own personal healing for so long. I would say to myself, "Well other people have it so much worse than I do, so I should just be happy with the way things are." Meanwhile, I was stressed, striving, and trying to control things I had no business trying to control.

Intellectualizing and rationalizing are tricky mechanisms. It can be easy to talk yourself out of something. Verbalizing your logic to another person might even make sense to that other person. Oftentimes our rationale is true. Yes, it was true that other people had worse situations than I had. But that does not mean I am not entitled to hurt feelings, nor that my wounds were unimportant. Yet connecting with those wounds made me feel insignificant, vulnerable, and useless. Rather than experiencing those emotions, I talked my way out of my feelings. I kept myself in "thinking mode" much of the time.

It is crucial to understand that "thinking" and "feeling" are two completely different experiences. In fact, we know from brain science that it is not possible to be emotional and logical at the same time. These processes occur in very different places in the brain. Engaging the thinking part of the brain quiets the emotional part. We cannot simultaneously experience a strong emotion *and* be logical and rational at the same time. If you are really stressed out or overwhelmed, your brain goes through changes that block your ability to engage the logic portion of your mind. This explains why people make bad decisions when they are emotional.

Of course, God has given us negative emotions for a reason. They are a marker, an indicator, and a sign that something in our environment is wrong. Emotions are a gift. They signal an opportunity for us to reflect on why the current situation has triggered an emotion inside of us. This would allow us to take that situation directly to God so He can teach us His truth from that early situation.

But because we, as humans, try to manage the emotions ourselves with these defense mechanisms, we push away the one thing – our emotions – that could possibly lead us to our healing. Intellectualization is one of the more challenging defenses to break down. However, the reward for tackling this personal challenge makes the effort so worthwhile.

You learned some of the mental gymnastics people use to avoid connecting with deep emotional pain. However, sometimes these defense mechanisms do not fully do their job. Sometimes unpleasant and uncomfortable emotions still arise and plague us. This is when we start to bring in the more powerful ways of escaping our feelings – coping mechanisms. And these can create significant problems.

Coping Mechanisms

You now know the basics of the various mental tricks we use in order to avoid unpleasant emotions that develop in us during situations that trigger our wounded hearts. We deploy these defense mechanisms automatically to make the bad feelings disappear.

The problem is that oftentimes our mental gymnastics do not do the full job. Sometimes they only push a portion of the pain away, or we have so many issues that our minds simply cannot keep up with the negative events. This puts us in a real bind – our primary objective is to make unpleasant emotions go away. When our minds cannot do the job, we turn to other options. And here is where some major problems start to crop up.

You may have heard the term "retail therapy." Women often use this phrase to describe the way they handle a tough situation – they head to the local mall to spend some money. The excursion is for the specific purpose of creating distance between a tough situation and our emotional response. As a way of avoiding or pushing our feelings to the back of our minds, we break out the credit card and head to the mall.

Or, maybe after a long day at work, you arrive home to discover that your children are particularly whiny, needing more of your attention than you have the energy to give. You know your aggravation is not their problem, and you certainly do not want to take it out on them. So, to get through the rest of the evening, you pour yourself an extra glass of wine. Or maybe two extra glasses. It helps take the edge off, and you can interact more calmly with your children until their bedtime.

Perhaps your husband starts withdrawing emotionally from you, maybe even giving you the silent treatment. Or he spends more time at work lately on an important project. Although you understand why he is not home, you feel lonely and even as if his work is more important than you. You know it does not make sense to feel rejected, but you cannot seem to keep those terrible feelings from creeping in. That gallon of ice cream tastes great. Those potato chips in the cabinet are easy to eat in front of the television while you binge-watch a 90s sitcom on Netflix.

In more extreme cases, the leftover pain medication in your medicine cabinet does a great job of erasing the hurt of rejection and loneliness. What harm in only taking one or two, since you are alone in the house anyway? Or as your anxiety levels creep up, you start to feel your tension rise, your heart starts to pound, and your jitteriness increases. You experience uneasiness and worry about the unknown. To make the feeling go away, you reach for the anti-anxiety prescription your doctor gave you a few weeks ago to help you "ride out" these moments.

Intense emotional experiences make us respond in ways to quench them as quickly as possible. Unfortunately, most of what we choose works well and works fast. Food soothes us almost immediately. Alcohol, drugs, and other substances blunt our senses, creating an illusion of everything being "okay."

Because our coping strategies do a fine job of making unpleasant emotions disappear quickly, we are rewarded for using them. That means the next time we have rising anxiety, disappointment, rejection, or discouragement, we will remember how easy it is to handle them. We again reach for the credit card, the junk food, or the drugs and alcohol to smooth over the issue. The internet has created new categories of maladaptive coping strategies – pornography, excessive use of social media, and the online world of alternate identities. People can create avatars – a symbol of themselves or how they would like to be – and interact in virtual worlds online with other people. These alternate worlds allow people to indulge in activities they might not do in the real world (like flirt with other people, have simulated relationships with other avatars, and act out fantasies and situations that may not be healthy).

We all have coping mechanisms. Mine is eating sugary foods. Regardless of the specific way of managing unpleasant emotions, these coping styles can escalate into very severe situations. Most addictions start out as innocent ways of coping with life. Because the drug of choice (including food, or even sexual behavior) makes the bad feelings go away rapidly, these behaviors become entrenched. Over time, they become strongholds. We gravitate to the substance or the behavior – the wine or the shopping – instead of tackling tough issues head-on. Avoidance becomes not only easy but really rewarding.

Our coping mechanism of choice can become obvious to others. We gain weight, or we withdraw from friends in favor of our online "friends." Our real-world relationships suffer as the alcohol or drugs take priority over human connection. And they certainly take a higher place in life over God. After all, it is much easier to light up a joint than it is to open a Bible, read several verses, ask God to speak to you, and then wait to hear Him. Passively allowing a substance to overtake your conscious mind take far less effort than pursuing God.

Can you see Satan in this process?

The defenses and coping strategies we deploy do not work, except to deceive us into believing they do work. They keep up separated from the very thing we want the most – love, acceptance, and contentment. Those defenses we use not only keep us from fully connecting with other people at a heart level (because our hearts believe that by fully connecting with someone, we will then be vulnerable to inevitable hurt), those defenses keep us from God, too!

God knows all of this about us. While He sees us on a path *not* of His choosing, He allows us to stay on it because that is what we want to do. He respects our free will, and He loves us enough not to impose Himself and force us to do something else.

But all along, He tries to get our attention, tries to get us to look to Him for guidance, support, direction, and love. Every day, all day, He puts things in our paths that could trigger us to stop, be still, and turn to Him for guidance. We either fail to recognize those moments because we are too busy doing "other" things, or we do recognize them and choose to ignore them (maybe because we really like the path we are on – that alcohol makes us feel good momentarily, and yelling at our children gives us the brief illusion of having control and power over someone else, and watching reality television shows make us feel better about ourselves as we sit and pass judgment on someone else's choices). We are attached to our coping strategies because we have agreed with the deception that, because they make us "feel good" for a moment, our problems are gone.

God honors the fact that we choose to believe this illusion, even when He lovingly wants something better for us. It is only when we decide to finally still ourselves, and *know* that He is God, that He can pluck us off that path, and gently settle us down onto the path that He wants us to follow. This is what the healing words of God achieve in an instant. POOF! We know in that moment when God speaks intimately, lovingly, and directly to our hearts, or when He shows us an image of something so beautiful and meaningful that we automatically shift onto the new path He has for us.

No matter what earthly or fleshly option you choose to help you cope with life, the goal is to yield to Christ as the source for your emotional needs. Remember what Biblical stillness is – it is the deliberate cessation of striving, a full and total surrender and submission to Him, in quiet and peace. In this still posture, we can allow God to transform our hearts. This process does not happen quickly, but it does reliably happen once we give it some attention. God wants us to approach Him willingly. He will reward our movements toward Him ("Draw near to God and He will draw near to you," James 4:8).

This requires a willingness to resist the strong pull toward the things that have, in the past, been reliable "remedies" of our pain. When we purpose putting Him first, it means we plan on riding out the temptations and cravings that will happen. Those cravings will be intense. You will need to rely even more on God to overcome them. The temptations will come from both physical and spiritual sources. But when we submit both our physical and spiritual challenges to God, He will respond. Do not expect this process to happen smoothly and seamlessly. The devil has been working in your life for some time, getting you to believe that his ways work, and because they are easy and "feel good," they are the best option. "Resist the devil and he will flee from you," James tells us in 4:7. Be still, and know that He is God.

I promise that you will never regret this path of healing. You will encounter bumps and detours, but each step along the way, your heart will experience deeper levels of growth and restoration. Yes, we do some destructive behaviors, but God is faithful.

We know God has a plan for you and that the enemy wants to thwart that plan by attacking your heart. When your heart is wounded, you have too many anxieties, worries, discouragements, and hang-ups to pursue God's purpose in your life. I know you are eager to claim this victory over your emotional pain and move forward! But there is one more detail you need to understand before learning and practicing being still, and it involves all these defense and coping mechanisms you just learned about.

Chapter Eight: Was Jesus Wrong?

I have a confession to make. Even though I had yielded my heart to Christ years ago, until my 40-day fasting experience, I carried a major doubt in my mind about one of the central tenants of the Christian faith. Regardless of how long you have been a Christ-follower, you probably know the following set of commandments confirmed by Jesus:

> And you shall love the Lord your God will all your heart, with all your soul, with all your mind, and with all your strength. This is the first commandment. And the second, like it, is this: You shall love your neighbor as yourself. There is no other commandment greater than these. (Mark 12:30-31)

> This is My commandment, that you love one another as I have loved you. (John 15:12)

Many people refer to this concept of "loving thy neighbor" as the golden rule. The idea is that we are to treat other people as we expect to be treated. This admonition certainly makes sense on the surface. We want others to be kind to us, so we should be kind to others. We want others to respect us, so we should respect others.

Here was my problem: I knew, for a fact, that many people expect others to treat them poorly. A large percentage of people believe that others are out to harm them. They lack trust in their fellow man and believe that they are vulnerable to harm. While we do not *want* others to disappoint us or to let us down or to take advantage of us, some of us live on high alert for this mistreatment to happen. We expect it, or at least we assume there is a likelihood that someone will hurt us. The truth is that very few people love themselves. And if we do not love ourselves, how can we properly love other people?

Growing up with a wounded heart causes us to hold others at a distance, and to work overtime to protect that heart from further wounding. The defense and coping mechanisms form a virtual "wall" around our hearts. This wall is meant to keep us safe. If we do not give people access to our hearts, then our hearts will not be hurt. Or so we believe.

We learned in the last chapter that our human efforts fail at their job. We cannot protect ourselves by distorting reality or medicating the pain away. The wound persists and will continually bring up negative emotions until permanent healing happens. That wall around our hearts gives us the illusion of protection. In reality, that wall keeps us distant from the two things we want the most: relationship with others, and to feel accepted by God. The wall keeps God out of our hearts.

How can we give love to others when we have such a limited amount in our own hearts? That defensive wall around your heart grows thicker each time someone hurts your feelings and you fall back on a defense or a coping strategy. Not only does this keep your wound intact, but it also keeps your heart less and less engaged with other people.

In therapy, I routinely heard about men and women who tolerated abuse, neglect, disrespect, or simple disinterest from a spouse or other important person in their lives. In no way do I mean that they "allowed" the bad treatment, but they were so beaten down emotionally that they believed they deserved that kind of treatment. How, then, could Jesus have the audacity to say we are to treat others the way we want to be treated? If we believe we deserve others treating us so poorly, that does not bode well for His expectations of us with others.

This did not make sense to me. Why would Christ *command us* to do the one thing that is guaranteed to hurt others? Here I will admit to my own insecurity – as much as this bothered me, I never spoke my doubt out loud to anyone else. I was embarrassed, and concerned that someone would say, "Well, duh, Anita! You are supposed to rise above your own 'stuff' and treat others properly no matter your personal situation.'"

So I kept my mouth shut....until the Lord revealed yet another powerful truth during my fast. He showed me exactly how all of this fits together. We have a wounded heart, and our defense and coping mechanisms create the spiritual equivalent of a wall around our hearts. That wall not only keeps us distanced from other people, but it also keeps God at a distance.

With our hearts walled off from God, we are not able to experience His full love for us. We cannot properly receive His perfect love because of the defenses we have built and maintained around our hearts. While Jesus commanded us to love others as we wish to be loved, it was His second commandment. His first was to love the Lord our God with all of our hearts, minds, souls, and strength. If our hearts are walled off, if we maintain a defensive posture with everyone – including God – we cannot love Him with everything we have. Our defenses are meant to protect us from giving away more of our hearts, so we keep them protected behind this spiritual wall. While I know you love God, you most likely hold back in your love toward Him because that wall is a barrier.

Not only do we all fail to love God with everything in us because we are so distracted by our futile attempts at keeping our hearts "safe," that spiritual wall prevents our hearts from receiving God's love. This is important – we love Him because He loved us first (1 John 4:19). If we do not allow His love into our hearts, then where can our love come from?

This explains why your personal healing is so crucial. When you allow God to heal your wounded heart, you will also allow more of His love to flood into your newly healed heart. From that point, you can more powerfully and properly love others according to His commandment. But we must first attend to the most important commandment – love God with everything in us by allowing His love into our hearts. That love we are to direct toward God must originate from somewhere. Despite the "self-love" movement, it is actually impossible to generate love on our own. That love must come from somewhere, and it does! That love we direct to God and others *comes from God Himself.*

The command to love God first has a "first fruits" quality to it. When we receive His love, the first thing we do is return it back to Him. Then we turn it to others. With that spiritual defensive wall up around our hearts, we block God's love from entering in. This is why hurting people hurt others. We treat people out of the remnants of what is in our hearts, and it isn't much. We exhaust it quickly and then have no more patience or love for anyone else.

Imagine my thrill when I realized that – shockingly – Jesus Christ was not wrong! We read those verses without understanding the fullness of what they mean, and what we need to do in order to live out those commands. Jesus is not mistaken. He was teaching us the process of how this all works: love God by receiving His love for us, then our hearts are filled up with His love, which we can then direct toward others, and ourselves, in a godly way.

Be clear on what your role is in this process. That wall around your heart that you have carefully crafted for years is only an illusion. It does not keep you safe, although you believe it does. The most damaging effect it has, though, is keeping God out of your heart. For God to heal your heart, you must allow Him access to it. Sometimes this is hard. If you believe that God let you down in the past, or if you have anger toward Him for not saving you from something, then allowing Him into your heart (and mind) could sound scary. But He will not force Himself on you. Letting Him in will be a deliberate decision on your part. Being still is how you will do it.

While you may feel like this is a big risk, it is not. Remember, there is no condemnation in Christ. God is not mad at you, He has not abandoned you, He has not forsaken you. He loves you with an everlasting love (Jer 31:3). He made you. He has your name inscribed on the palm of His hand (Isa 49:16). He chose you before He established the foundation of the earth (Eph 1:4). God formed you in your mother's womb (Ps 139:13; Isa 44:2; Jer 1:4; Job 31:15).

These verses speak the truth. You may have had bad things happen to you, and because you were young and vulnerable, you mistook the actions of people for the intentions of God. We all do this to some extent. We think we want God to exert His power in our lives and prevent bad things from happening. However, it simply is impossible in this fallen world. He *will* provide that protection for us in heaven. But until then, we are called to be His disciple, to allow Him to be Lord of our lives so we can walk in His will according to His purposes in a fallen, sinful world.

Jesus was not wrong when he told us to treat others as we wish to be treated. He also told us to love one another as He loves us. Therefore, we need to receive and experience His love for us. This will permit us to love others in the way He wants, not in our limited way from a wounded heart.

Meditate upon these verses about who you are. Give God access to your heart to bring to your awareness the lies your heart believes. When you do, you prime your heart for His loving healing. This healing happens with His direct, intimate communication with your heart.

God's speech carries weight, not just in terms of its truth and gravity, but in its depth and breadth. One three-word sentence – "You are Mine," or "I love you" – can set straight a lifetime of hurt and pain. The weight of God's words will redeem lost time, resurrect dead dreams, and restore damaged hearts, minds, and relationships.

Words that achieve those results are indeed weighty because of the force, power, and, sovereignty they carry. His words directed into your mind and heart have a lovingly corrective impact, gently telling you where you have believed things about yourself, about Him, and about the world that are wrong or misguided. He sets you straight with love, compassion, and caring. It is the most beautiful thing to witness – it is like watching a rebirth of a human being, a person being translated from their previous world of hopelessness, pain, and captivity, into a light-filled world of truth, love, acceptance, and freedom.

God's words are expansive. They help you understand the narrowness of how you have been viewing yourself and your life, as well as how you have assumed God to be restrictive and contained. Our God is *power*. He *created power*! Think about that for a moment. The loving Creator of the universe generated the concept of power, something that makes our world function and move without us even understanding one bit of how it works. He can pick us up off the path we are on that is wrong, misguided, and chosen based on our futile attempts to avoid more emotional hurts and pain.

Because our hearts are broken, we spend gargantuan amounts of time trying to defend them against getting hurt even further. We think if we withhold ourselves from interacting with certain people, or if we allow ourselves to get offended by people or ideas, or if we simply try to avoid certain circumstances, then our hearts will stay whole. Then we will not experience more hurt and pain.

Now you know that our human attempts simply do not work. But God does work. God loves us. We allow ourselves to receive God's love, which fills our hearts with healing truth. Then we can turn around and use that love to shower onto others. This is the way it works. Skewed versions of spirituality encourage you to "love yourself." Self-love makes no sense at all. Where does the love that one is supposed to direct to one's self originate from? God is love (1 John 4:8). So any love we direct toward anyone, including ourselves, must come from God through His Son Jesus Christ. Trying to "love yourself" apart from God is counterfeit. Of course, we can respect ourselves and establish and maintain proper life boundaries.

But love? It must come from God. We allow that love into our hearts by cracking open the carefully constructed walls around our hearts. That love flows in, healing the wounds and correcting the lies you believe. As our hearts fill with His love for us, our wounds heal, we become stronger in the Lord, and can then love others as He loves us. This is the only way we can obey His command.

And it all starts with being still. Read on to find out how to be still and put yourself inside the Ultimate Healer.

Chapter Nine: The Nuts and Bolts – How to Be Still

Sophia came into my office and I could practically feel the waves of frustration coming from her. Last week, she and I had discussed the importance of becoming physically and mentally still, and I gave her some strategies to work on. As she sat down, she started talking before I even had time to ask her how she was doing.

"Well, I tried everything you suggested. And nothing happened. I sat in my chair and waited for God to speak to me and He didn't. I think I'm not meant to hear from Him," Sophia lamented.

"Okay, can you tell me what happened when you worked on the things we discussed?" I asked. We proceeded to talk through her prayer process and what happened as she implemented the suggestions I made to her. It turned out that she had two issues working against her ability to hear God's voice. First, her prayer time had to end at a specific time because she had to leave for work. It was difficult for her to relax and enter into intense prayer time when, in the back of her mind, she worried that she would get distracted and not leave her house on time. Second, she remained on what I call "high alert." Mentally, she was searching for God's voice, almost like scanning her mind and her environment to detect something. I find myself in this position frequently, so I understood Sophia's specific challenge.

I want to be honest with you right now. God does speak to people, every day, and in ways that each of us can properly hear and understand Him. He will never contradict Himself. He will not fail you.

Learning to be still and hear God will be a journey. For some readers, you will find you can move into stillness relatively quickly. For other readers, you may find it takes weeks of learning how to quiet your mind, slow down your thinking, and allow yourself to be in an emotional place of submission to God.

I urge you to never give up! It may not occur immediately, and in fact, may take some concerted effort. If you have any kind of control-related issues, including anxiety, then please extend yourself some mercy as it may take some time to turn the volume down on your own mental chatter and feel comfortable enough to release your perception of control. These are necessary components of being still, but they may initially feel scary or threatening. Just keep trying. At some point, you may want to consult a licensed and trusted Christian mental health provider who can help you navigate this process. Talking to others helps us unwind the tangles in our minds.

I say all of this because I want to make sure you do not believe that God rejected you or is uninterested in you. These are lies directly from Satan. The truth is that God loves you and wants to communicate with you. It is also true that you have spent many years trying to manage your hurts and pains in your own power. You have built up and nurtured habitual ways of thinking about other people and yourself, and about God. These beliefs feel comfortable and safe because you have fallen back on them for decades.

The idea of letting down these carefully crafted defenses might scare you or make you feel vulnerable. While these reactions are normal and understandable, they are wrong. When you expose yourself to God, you put yourself in the safest place in the entire universe. You are not exposing your deepest, darkest secrets to another person who might be untrustworthy. No, you are admitting the lies you believe about yourself to the One power and authority who is faithful, trustworthy, and loving. And oh, by the way, He already knows everything about you, anyway!

Sometimes other people have hurt us so deeply that we develop doubts about God's character. We mistake the failures of people with the actions of God. So many people act out of accordance with God's will and purpose. Sometimes those actions impact and hurt others. We have all been wounded because of other people acting outside of God's will. There is no way to escape this reality until we are with God in heaven.

Therefore, it is crucial that you understand the difference between humans and God. Yes, it may feel risky to trust God with your heart if you never have before. But what "feels" true can be untrue. We think that because we cannot trust people, we cannot trust God. If a loving God allowed other people to harm us, then we cannot trust God now.

The truth is God has always been with you, even in your darkest moments. He has sustained you, even when others were violating or abusing you. Yes, these things happened to you for reasons we cannot know or understand on this side of heaven. We have never been promised a perfect, pain-free life. He only promises He is there with us in our hard times, and we can trust Him to see us through.

> When you pass through the waters, I will be with you; And through the rivers, they shall not overflow you. When you walk through the fire, you shall not be burned, Nor shall the flame scorch you. (Isa 43:2)

> Yea, though I walk through the valley of the shadow of death, I will fear no evil; For You are with me; Your rod and Your staff, they comfort me. (Ps 23:4)

As painful and unpleasant as many life experiences are, we are never told we will avoid them. God tells us He knows the fallen condition of His creation, and because He loves us, He will remain with us and never leave us nor forsake us. When you consider your level of readiness to drop your defenses and allow the sovereign God of the universe to speak directly, intimately, and lovingly to your heart, know that He has been by your side every step of the way. He knows what happened to you, how you responded, and how you have tried to fix the problem in your own power. He is ready to take over if you allow Him. It starts with being still.

The Goal: Let us begin by remembering the goal you work toward. What does "stillness" mean? What does it look like? Here is a summary from chapter five. Stillness is a positional state of being in which we recognize who He is, as distinct from who we are. *Raphah* stillness is quite comprehensive and includes the following:

- A cessation of striving
- Being physically still (unmoving)
- Not allowing yourself to fight
- Not allowing yourself to try
- Not allowing yourself to search for answers
- Not allowing yourself to move, physically or mentally
- Acknowledge your weakness, relative to God's all-powerful strength
- Lowering your defenses
- Releasing the need to understand and know
- Releasing the need to continue seeking and being on high alert
- Humbling yourself, lowering yourself
- Leaving things alone
- Showing yourself slack, demonstrating your limitations
- Not allowing stress, overwhelm, worries, or fears to be in your mind at all
- Surrender
- Submission, recognizing that you are limited and God is limitless; you are powerless, and He is all-powerful

While your mind and body will be still, you will also mentally place yourself in a state of submission to God and God alone. You will be in proper alignment with Him, knowing your place relative to His place. A safer, more secure place you will never find. From this mental and spiritual stance, you can *know God.* You will experience the most profound understanding of Him and relationship with Him. From this posture, His communication with you will heal you. Remember, we find the healer inside of being still (*rapha* is within the word *raphah*).

Slowing down and stilling yourself in this powerful manner requires time and space. For most people, this is not accomplished by jamming it into "free moments" during your day. Stillness cannot be done frantically or quickly. However, after embarking on this journey, you will get to the point of being able to still your mind and body much more quickly. But these first few attempts need time and space.

The strategies you will read and practice will help you transition your mind from being in a highly active and striving state to being still. You can think of this process like taking a vacation to a relaxing tropical island. In order to transition from your normal hectic lifestyle to sitting on that tropical beach, you must first drive to an airport, board a plane, and fly to that island. In between your normal life and the relaxing vacation life you want exists a series of steps that help you bridge the gap between where you are and where you want to be.

These techniques serve the same purpose. When you practice them, the objective is to determine which strategies help you to wind down the mental chatter and tension and enter into biblical stillness. These strategies alone do not produce stillness. They simply act as activities to help you shift the state of your mind. If you have young children, you probably know that having a bedtime routine helps them ease into sleep. This happens because the routine tasks of getting into pajamas, reading a bedtime story, and brushing teeth signals their minds that it is time to wind down and prepare for sleep.

I want you to look at your journey of being still as just that – a journey. I will give you examples of strategies that have been proven to work to achieve *raphah* stillness. Not every suggestion will work for every person. Consider embarking on this journey as an experimental process. This means you will try some of these suggestions to evaluate whether they work for you or not.

Remove the sense of urgency and need to "get it right" from your mindset. Your relationship with God, and knowing who He is, develops and deepens with time. Whatever initial progress you make in your first few attempts will lay a foundation for your future relationship with the Lord. Time will march forward, so take the pressure off yourself to think you must achieve some level of stillness as quickly as possible. You do not. Keep pressing into God, keep taking the next step to knowing Him, and you will indeed know Him.

This means you must intentionally carve out time and space. You probably will need more than your normal quiet time. The exact amount of time you will need varies from person to person. As a guideline, consider starting with one hour sometime in the next week. If that is too much time (because I know, for instance, how crazy life can be if you have a toddler at home or are taking care of a medically ill family member), then take this opportunity to figure out what amount of time is reasonable, and what support systems you need to put in place to accomplish that amount of time.

For instance, some people have about an hour one time a week. They get up very early on a Saturday or Sunday (before their children wake up) and pursue stillness. Other people can insert almost daily time, but they too must wake up early to make their pursuit of stillness a reality. Sometimes you may need to find a babysitter or arrange for a family member to watch your children for you. Or perhaps you need to leave your house and go to another location that is quiet, or at least less intrusive. I have a client who would go sit in her car in her driveway to create a more conducive atmosphere to hearing God! Perhaps you can go to a beautiful park nearby or sit in a corner of a coffee shop. You may have to try a few options to find what works best for you.

I wish I could say that you can accomplish stillness in only 15 minutes. A few people might but most will not. The ability to have dedicated, extended time to create biblical stillness lies at the core of healing. This is not meant to make you hopeless if you simply do not have the time! But it does mean it will probably take you a bit longer to unwind the chatter in your mind and put yourself into this submissive, passive state. Another option to consider is if you only have your "normal" 15 minutes of quiet time, for instance, is that you can use this same amount of time in a very different way than you normally do. Spend that time implementing the strategies listed here, rather than defaulting to your standard devotional or Bible time.

Regardless of your specific time availability or constraints, prioritize the pursuit of stillness in whatever time and space you have. Look for extended chunks of time and commit to yourself to use them for stilling yourself to know that He is God. He honors all our efforts to reach out to Him and to press into Him.

Ten Strategies for Achieving Stillness

Once you have carved out the time and space to be still, the next step is to work on perhaps the hardest part of this process – getting rid of all the mental chatter in your mind. That chatter and internal dialogue churn in your brain, demanding your attention and energy. But in stillness, we learn to disregard that action, tame it, and even make those thoughts obedient to Christ. Making this happen requires patience and continued effort.

First, you want to ensure you are physically still. While this seems obvious and possibly even "easy," you might find yourself surprised at how fidgety and antsy you become as you start to turn the volume down on your mental chatter. For some people, doing exercise before your quiet time really helps. Discharging your physical energy beforehand and creating some physical fatigue can facilitate both body and mental stillness. Take a moment to consider if this might be helpful to you. Does it make sense for you to perhaps take a walk or fit in a quick workout before your "stillness time?" If you are not sure, then you may want to test it out. Perhaps for a few days, perform the experiment of walking for 20 minutes before you sit down to be still. See if this makes a difference for you.

Once you are physically still (and of course this means being physically comfortable, too, so sit in a good chair, adjust the room temperature so you feel warm or cool enough), then turn your attention to all the stuff in your mind. Your goal is to quiet that chatter. There are several techniques you can try, and then use the one (or more) that seem to help the most.

One: Dump list – This option has a rather unpleasant name, but it perfectly describes the action involved. Take about 10 minutes to "dump" everything in your mind onto paper. Write out all the things, both big and small, that occupy space in your mind. Please write this down physically on paper and resist the urge to type it. Physical writing forces your brain to slow down because it takes longer to write something than it does to type it.

What should be on this list? Anything and everything that goes through your mind! This means things as mundane as the things you want to remember to pick up at the grocery store, all the way to worrying about your child driving for the first time by him/herself…and it won't even happen for another year. But if it is something you worry about or think about or concern yourself with, then write it down.

I suggest 10 minutes because, in my experience, most people can write down a few of the more major things on their minds in the first minute or so. If you stop at that point, you will miss most things that roll through your mind so automatically that you almost forget how much emotional energy they consume. For instance, I am in a chronic battle with piles of paper on my desk. It really bothers me how easily and quickly my desk almost vomits out the papers that accumulate on it. But for some reason, I do not take the time to fix the problem (or at least I fail to do it as frequently as I "should"). Every day I sit at my desk to work, and it bothers me to have all these piles around me. Yet I put off the task so I can do other, more "important" things. Those piles really bug me and sometimes make me wonder what is wrong with ME that I continually allow it to happen.

This is an example of something that creates negative emotions in my mind on an almost daily basis, and because it is so chronic and such an integrated part of my daily experience, I tend to forget just how much angst it causes. It is not until I really start to ask myself, "What do I think about and worry about every day" that this issue crops up.

We all have these sorts of things. Maybe you worry about your kids' future. Perhaps you have a pile of clothes that needs to get to the dry cleaner and you keep forgetting to do it. Or maybe you have a family conflict that causes you pain and discouragement. Really think about everything that bothers you, no matter how massive or minuscule the issue.

And write them all down in at least 10 minutes. Sometimes it can take more than 10 minutes. If you have the time, then take it! It is very common the first time someone does a dump list that it takes more like 20 minutes. Typically, subsequent dump lists do not take as long as the first one. Therefore, if you think this may be the case for you, consider doing your first dump list at a time separate from your quiet time. Grab half an hour when you can and get all of this stuff onto paper. Then, when you do sit for quiet time, it will not take as long to get out the mental troubles because you will have already done the bulk of the work at an earlier time.

Regardless of how you use dump lists, I highly recommend them for easing your way into stillness. Sometimes we make the mental error of believing that we have to keep everything in our minds, even the issues that cause us worry and anxiety. This is simply not true. Writing down your worries in a big list has a therapeutic impact on your mind. Trying to keep everything juggled in your brain causes more stress and overwhelm. Simply discharging it all onto paper brings almost immediate relief.

I want to caution you – this exercise is about listing all the things in your mind. Resist the urge to write about each item. If you have a troubled marriage, write that down. But avoid making this a journaling exercise in which you explore the nuances of the problems and how you feel about everything. This is meant to be a list-making endeavor, not a journaling one. Remember, the goal is to turn the volume down on your mental chatter. The dump list helps you do this by taking issues out of your mind, and onto paper.

Two: Praying out loud – For some people, this suggestion will seem like an old habit. Many people routinely pray out loud. For others, it will feel strange and awkward. The objective is stillness, which means you eventually want to be silent. But you can aid the transition to silence by praying out loud. Personally, I find this to be extremely effective. Sometimes when I pray only in my mind, I lose track of what I pray about. My mind can wander easily if I allow it. But praying out loud makes it easier to stay on target and keep focus. It also forces you to slow down your thinking, which powerfully helps move you toward stillness.

If you do not regularly pray out loud, and you have self-consciousness about it, I recommend trying it out a few times in your car while driving. Turn off your radio and pray to God. Move down your prayer list – whatever it is – and simply practice praying out loud. You will feel more comfortable with this the more you do it.

When you pray out loud, pray for 10 minutes. Remember, the goal is to empty your mind of all your stuff. Taking your anxieties, worries, burdens for other people, and prayer requests from your prayer list and putting them onto God effectively removes them from your brain. Just like with the dump list, you want to take the cares of your mind and cast them onto God. You want to resist complaining or harping about issues. God knows the entirety of your circumstances, so resist the urge to hang onto an issue.

Always remember the objective to turn down the volume of mental chatter, stop striving for answers, or to feel heard, or to prove anything to God or anyone else. Dial back and stop trying. The only way you can allow God to hold on to your concerns is if you let go of them. He will not wrestle them away from you. Release them and move on.

Three: Deep breathing – This practice powerfully shifts your mind (and your body) away from stress, anxiety, worry, and overwhelm and into a calmer and more relaxed state. Biblical stillness does not necessarily mean "relaxed," but I use that term as a way of counterbalancing the tension associated with an active, occupied mind.

When we are stressed or tense, or simply going through the day-to-day motions, our breathing tends to be shallow and rapid. The consequences of breathing this way include increased muscle tension, cold hands and feet, higher blood pressure, and an increased heart rate. Plus, stress hormones release into your bloodstream, impacting other internal body organs as well as the brain. In fact, when we are stressed, it becomes impossible for our brain to access the frontal lobe. This is a problem because the frontal lobe drives our ability to think logically, plan for the future, and make rational decisions.

Shifting away from stress breathing has an immediate impact on the body and the brain. When we slow down our breathing, blood pressure starts to decrease, as does the heart rate and muscle tension. Since deep breathing costs no money, can be done anywhere, and does not have harmful side effects, it is a wonderful way to begin reducing the mental clutter and chatter.

When you practice deep breathing, keep in mind two main words: slow and controlled. You want to both slow your breathing down and to control your breath. This makes deep breathing different from a sigh. A sigh involves taking in more oxygen, but also releasing it rather quickly. There is no harm at all in this, but it does not have the impact on your mind and body that deep breathing has.

For a deep breath, you want to inhale slowly, then exhale slowly. To make it simple, I suggest counting in your mind as you inhale and exhale. On the inhale, count to three, then on your exhale, count to three or four.

The exact numbers do not matter. I only suggest them as a way of helping you understand what a slow breath feels like. Also, counting in your mind helps to take the focus away from the normal things bouncing around your brain and gives you something simple and calm toward which to direct your attention. Therefore, counting serves many helpful purposes, but it is not required to do this practice.

You may have heard of diaphragmatic breathing. This is also referred to as "belly breathing," and it means you shift the focus from using your lungs to breathe to using your diaphragm to control your breathing. A sign that you have made this shift is that you see can see your belly expand when you inhale and then retract when you exhale. There is some advantage to belly breathing because using your diaphragm expands your lungs to a greater capacity, thereby bringing more oxygen into your bloodstream. While belly breathing does enhance deep breathing, it is not required to obtain the benefits of it.

Deep breathing, while simple, is probably one of the better ways of transitioning into stillness. You will get an immediate physical relaxation effect, and your mind will seem calmer almost right away. I highly recommend giving this a try!

Four: Worship music for a short period of time – Listening to worship music can move you into a stronger sense of the presence of God. Popping your earbuds in and choosing your favorite worship song gives your mind something godly to focus on rather than the worries and fears that often dominate the modern mind. It can powerfully move you into a more contemplative mode.

However, the key is to use this music only for a short time. Remember, the objective is to be still. This means keeping just about all mental chatter to a minimum. While worship music and hymns insert the Word of God into your mind, focusing on the lyrics can also be a form of distraction. The lyrics serve as an external source of attention for your brain.

Having instrumental, non-lyrical music can help form another bridge between the frantic state of mind into stillness. You can listen to lyrical worship music and then shift to non-lyrical music. YouTube has instrumental versions of popular worship songs that you might want to check out for this purpose.

I often have the sounds of the ocean as background noise. Biblical stillness is a state of mind, not necessarily "silence." If having background noise really helps you, the key is finding something that serves as white noise and does not direct your attention. You want to turn down the volume of your thoughts, not just replace your thoughts with other thoughts (even godly ones). Needing to have something with words to focus on might distract you from hearing from God.

Of course, everyone is different! I would never want to make a blanket statement that no one should listen to worship music while trying to be still. But having worked with so many people, and knowing how most people's brains tend to function, I recommend non-lyrical songs as you transition into stillness. Try it a few times and see what happens.

Five: Physical activity – For some people, exercise or physical activity can help clear the mind. It is not necessary to be physically still in order to be mentally still, although most people find physical stillness to be a component of biblical stillness. Others, though, can reach that place of not striving, being calm and quiet, and in surrender to God while walking in nature. Some people can reach this state while driving a car.

You will have to do some trial and error with this. Walking or exercise, as long as you do not look at your phone constantly, can help burn off some stress. Some days I have to exercise before I can mentally turn things down. Most of the time I do not need to, but occasionally, I really need a workout before I can do my quiet time. Once you start trying things, you will become more attuned to how God created you to position yourself in stillness.

Related to physical activity, you may want to kneel. Kneeling is a humbling posture and can help you mentally surrender to God by physically demonstrating your humility during your prayer time. Matching physical posture to mental posture can accelerate the transition to *raphah* stillness.

Six: Doodling – Some people find doodling, drawing, or engaging in non-serious artwork helps facilitate stillness. Not being artistically inclined, I have no personal experience with this, but I have heard from numerous people that having pencils and a sketch pad nearby during their quiet time greatly helps them release the clutter in their mind in a way that dump lists cannot do for them. Since everyone is different, you may want to give this a try, especially if you tend to doodle during meetings or your downtime.

Seven: Meditating on the Word of God – Find a verse that really speaks to you and repeat it either in your mind or out loud. You eventually want to arrive at the place where you are not generating the thoughts in your head, and where you embrace the concept of not striving. But in this transition phase of moving from the busyness of your daily mind to the *raphah* stillness God tells us we can know from within, repeating a Bible verse over and over can help.

Some people combine this with praying out loud, and over time have found it to help more efficiently move into stillness. Remember that trial and error is required for you to determine which strategies most effectively help you.

Eight: Reading the Bible out loud – If, like me, you sometimes struggle with reciting even one Bible verse repeatedly out loud (in my case because my memory sometimes fails me!), then pick up the Bible, open up to a page, and start reading it out loud. I cannot emphasize how effective this strategy is, and how it can help you not only move toward *raphah* stillness but also can show you things in the Bible you never saw before. Hearing the Bible read out loud makes your brain absorb the same verse in a different way. The material enters your brain via different neural pathways than are used when you read the Bible.

Reading it out loud means you hear it as well as read it. You may find new revelations unfold as you practice this method. Even if you do not use this technique to be still, you can use it to deepen your understanding of the Word of God.

As for stillness, reading the Bible out loud forces the verse to take over your brain, which means the worrisome and bothersome stuff must retreat. Of course, it will help you put more Scripture into your mind, but it also can help with the transition process to stillness. To make this technique even more powerful, perhaps find a chapter in the Bible that speaks to the omnipotence and omniscience of God. Reading about how all-powerful He is can help make it easier to submit to His authority in *raphah* stillness. It can show you your place in relationship to His place.

Nine: Release physical tension – Sometimes we hold on to tension – physical and mental – because it helps give us the illusion that we are in control. We equate tension, and even anxiety and worry, with control. Release this tension by doing some stretching exercises. Letting go of physical tension can bring more mental relief, thus making stillness easier. My only caution would be to avoid yoga.

Yoga is a Hindu practice. The poses in yoga are meant to honor, acknowledge, or, in some cases, worship Hindu gods. I know that "Christian yoga" is popular, and many people have told me that they pray to Jesus while performing the poses. Of course, Christ is stronger and more powerful than any demonic force. However, I would not play around with a Ouija board or tarot cards even if they had the image of Jesus on them. Since God is the same yesterday, today, and forever, and since God has warned us repeatedly not to engage in the practices of the pagans, I would suggest you pray and ask God what He thinks about the practice of yoga.

Ten: Silence – This one might be tricky for some readers. Things come up when we are silent. At some point in your pursuit of stillness, you will want to sit in silence as a way of concentrating on your submission to the Lord God Almighty. If things come up in your mind as you sit in silence, write them down. Do not push them back into your mind or pretend like they are not there. Allow yourself to acknowledge them and continue.

Important points to remember:
- It may take several attempts over a few weeks or even months. Just keep at it. You will notice that each time you attempt stillness it gets easier. This is a process and a journey. Do not condemn yourself, feel discouraged, or believe you can "never" be still simply because it takes time to arrive at that place.
- Pay attention to "stuff" that comes up. The Lord may be allowing you to realize some tough truths – maybe you don't really trust Him, maybe you are angry at Him, maybe you blame Him. Whatever comes up, have courage and acknowledge it. Then turn around and take it back to Him. In prayer, say, "Lord, I know You want me to trust you, but I do not. I want to trust You, but I am scared. Lord, what do you want me to know?" Then wait for His answer.
- You want to be Mary, not Martha. I find it helps to have a visual picture of Mary sitting at the feet of Jesus Christ, completely receptive and in the full understanding of who He is, and who she is in relation. That is the state of mind you want to create.

- Be in a receptive state, not a mental place of tension, scanning, searching, high alert, or forcing something to happen. Submit, surrender, and stop striving.

One last point I need to make. Sometimes a life event will consume you to the point that you cannot be still, even when you have learned how to create that *raphah* stillness. This has happened to me. About a year ago, our family had a major crisis with a very close family member. I apologize for not telling details, but it is not my story to tell. I am limited to only telling my part in what happened.

It was life or death, and I was totally devastated. The crisis took me out spiritually and mentally. I was terrified and distressed. I tried to turn to God for comfort and I attempted to still my mind so I could hear a desperately needed word from Him. I simply could not silence my mind. Too much fear and pain consumed me.

I needed to take a more dramatic step in order to get myself in a posture in which I could hear from God. So I did the only thing left to do – I fasted. I fasted from food entirely for two days. And then I restricted my food intake to only fruits and vegetables for 10 days. I had to throw myself at the feet of the Almighty in the only way left I knew to do. It worked.

I was able to be still – and make no mistake about it, this "stillness" was not particularly peaceful or quiet. It was rather an extreme release of trying to control the uncontrollable, deep recognition that I was powerless, yet He is all-powerful, that I know almost nothing, and He knows everything.

He spoke to me in the same way He always does when I hear from Him with healing words: direct, loving, yet gentle. His input gave me incredible comfort and even resulted in a breakthrough for the person who was struggling. I am eternally grateful, and since that time I often reflect on how He answered my prayers in my desperation. He is faithful and true, even when things are not going the way I want them to. In fact, that is when I need Him the most, and when I need to deploy a more extreme tactic.

I mention this to you in case you spend months trying these strategies yet remain in a struggle with being still. As a last resort, please consider a time of fasting and praying. God honors all attempts to approach Him. Sometimes we need to do something that forces our own minds to be humble. Any activity that forces you to focus and concentrate on something that is not your own stuff, but on God and your position in relation to Him and who He is will bring you closer to Him.

Chapter Ten: Barriers to Healing

Having worked with hundreds of people in helping them still their minds for the purpose of hearing a direct, personal, intimate word from God regarding their deepest emotional wounds, I have seen evidence of blocked or delayed healing. I want to have caution in describing these barriers to healing because sometimes it can come across as "blaming the victim" when God remains silent with our requests to Him.

I have recognized a pattern in the healing process. The first time a person comes boldly to His throne for mercy and grace in time of need, and in *raphah* stillness, He heals with a profound, succinct word. When this happens, a portion of the wounded heart is made new again, as if it had never been wounded. Hallelujah!

However, when the person seeks the Lord again in the future, the word from the Lord seems distant and unattainable. This happened often enough that I prayed to the Lord on behalf of His people whom I serve for an answer. He then revealed in more depth the responsibility that each of us has in our own healing process.

When we pursue healing, eventually we will come up against an issue that He wants us to resolve in order to release further healing. We can put up blockades that have the impact of a spiritual barrier. It is not a matter of "blaming us" for our lack of healing, but rather a revelation of an area in which God wants our obedience. The Christian writer John Eldredge says repeatedly in his book, *Moving Mountains*, that "there is a way things work." Simply, God has established a process by which issues and events happen more smoothly. When we operate within His processes, we can expect more of what He wants for us. When we operate outside of His processes, things get jammed up. Our role is to maintain communion with the Lord so we can allow Him to nudge us closer and closer to His way of doing things.

This requires our active participation and a degree of responsibility in the healing journey. It is not a matter of us being "wrong" for doing, or not doing, something. Rather, it involves a simple truth that God has the resolution for our issues, and we either align ourselves within that truth or we do not. Please remember that there is no condemnation in Christ Jesus, so if you come to realize that you have inadvertently blocked healing because of one of these reasons, God is not mad at you! He simply has a revelation regarding something in your life about which He wants you to change your mind.

Let's examine three of those issues that function as barriers to healing, and how God wants you to change your mind.

Unforgiveness

In my opinion, having worked with people in various capacities of mental health and personal growth, the issue of unforgiveness is the single biggest barrier to healing (or really to forward movement of any kind). In fact, forgiveness is such a major issue that even the secular mental health field studies it scientifically.

Before we go forward with examining forgiveness and unforgiveness, I want to define the terms. Many people misunderstand what true forgiveness entails, and this misunderstanding only prolongs the spiritual, psychological, and even physical impact of unforgiveness.

Forgiveness is a process – or the result of a process – in which a person chooses to release feelings of offense, blame, anger, bitterness, resentment, and the need to punish a person (or group of people) who hurt, harmed, or otherwise acted unjustly toward them. When we are injured in some way (emotionally, physically, or spiritually) by another person, we naturally may experience anger and resentment toward the perpetrator. In many cases, the anger is not only understandable but also justified. People commit unfair and unjust acts every day against undeserving folks. Also, accidents happen that, while not intended to disrupt or even destroy another person's life, have that exact impact.

When you are treated poorly, you react with righteous indignation. The unfair event creates a wedge between you, the victim, and the perpetrator. The offensive experience pushes apart the people involved. This relational division is invisible yet also seems to have real substance. The anger and bitterness erect a virtual wall between the offender and the victim. This barrier may be understandable, and it even gives the victim a sense of control and power when they feel out of control and powerless.

But holding on to the sense of offense also has negative consequences. Research has shown that unforgiveness causes mental health problems such as depression and anxiety. Maintaining resentment, bitterness, and offense keeps you angry. And chronic anger increases the risk of heart disease, diabetes, high blood pressure, and chronic pain conditions. In short, unforgiveness carries with it a huge physical and emotional burden that is not without consequences.

In contrast, forgiveness calms stress levels, lowers your risk of heart disease, reduces physical pain, reduces blood pressure, and improves sleep. In fact, recent studies revealed a surprising finding that among people who have high levels of life stress, if a person has a high level of forgiveness, they have no increase in the risk of mental health problems. Forgiveness seems to protect our emotional health from the harmful effects of extreme life stress.

Clearly, even apart from God's thoughts on forgiveness, the pursuit of releasing the offense we hold against another person is a worthy one. So, why don't we forgive more easily and more often? Many people believe the wrong things about forgiveness, thinking it means something it does not.

For instance, forgiveness does not let the other person off the hook. When we forgive someone, we are not saying that what they did was okay, or that it was not harmful, and does not really matter anymore. It also does not mean we forget what happened. You can never forget, or erase from your memory, the unjust acts committed against you. However, you can learn to release feelings of anger, bitterness, resentment, and a need to see the other person punished. Sometimes people believe that withholding forgiveness functions as a type of punishment, or emotional payback or retribution. The thinking is, "By not forgiving you, I am punishing you by keeping you at arm's length and holding this against you." However, unforgiveness does not function like this.

There is a saying that holding onto unforgiveness is like taking poison and expecting it to kill your opponent. Your unforgiveness is *yours* to either hold on to or release. The person who wronged you might like to have your forgiveness, but it does not actually impact his or her life at all. You are the one who experiences the spiritual, physical, and emotional consequences of forgiveness – not the offender.

Forgiving someone does not absolve the need for justice. They may still have consequences to deal with. In some cases, the offender might not even express sorrow or regret for their behavior. This makes the forgiveness journey more challenging, but it still is important to release those negative feelings. When you forgive someone, that negativity is replaced with more empathy, peace, and possibly even compassion. After forgiveness, you can remember the event without having the negative feelings grip you like they did before. You can think of the person without wishing them harm or focusing on a grievance or revenge. The memory exists in the absence of emotional hurt.

Do not mistake forgiveness for trust, however. If someone abused you, you can forgive them without trusting them in the future. Your relationship can change and become more distant so that you no longer place yourself in a potentially abusive situation. This can happen even while you forgive them for past wrongdoings. While reconciliation is God's desire, the nature of the reconciled relationship can include proper boundaries and psychological defenses going forward.

In the natural realm, forgiveness comes with many health, emotional, and relational benefits. But the primary reason to forgive someone is that God wants you to forgive. In fact, forgiveness is a big deal in God's kingdom.

The entire reason we need Jesus Christ as our savior is because we must be forgiven. God has ordained that, for us to be reconciled to Him, our sins must be forgiven. We cannot pay restitution for our sins, so we cannot save ourselves spiritually. No amount of good deeds can erase or offset the marks on our souls from the things we have done over the course of our entire lives.

When I was eight years old, I stole some of my brother's Halloween candy. I knew it was wrong, so I took it secretly, when he wasn't looking. I also knew he was too young to really miss the candy. While I fessed up to my brother and he forgave me (years later, I might add!), when I face the judgment seat, that one event will still be a mark against me. Even if I never did anything else wrong in my life – if I never stole his candy when I was nine and ten years old, or even if I didn't steal my kids' candy when they were young – I still will be held accountable for that one infraction. But I have no way, in my own power, of paying the debt that is owed to God for sinning against him by stealing. I've got myself a problem.

Blessedly, I also have a savior, Jesus Christ, who died on the cross exactly for this purpose. He took the punishment for my sins. He sacrificed Himself to take a punishment that I could never fulfill, just so I can be reconciled to God Almighty. Thank you, Jesus, that when I face the judgment seat of God, I have You as my advocate and to stand in my place. I can claim Your blood, Jesus, as payment for my sins. I am eternally grateful!

God says my sins are as far as the east is from the west (Ps 103:12) because I am forgiven by the blood of Christ Jesus. I need forgiveness, and God provided a solution for me and for you. I want to prove through Scripture this fact because, as I mentioned earlier, I know many people who, although they want healing, they fear what God might say to them. They worry that God will condemn or belittle their life choices or will reject them. If you believe this or worry about it, please know that it is not true! When you understand how much God loves you – so much that He sacrificed His one and only Son so you can be with Him for eternity – you will feel more comfortable approaching His throne.

And remember – He did this all because we desperately need forgiveness of our wrongdoings. We deserve punishment for our wrongdoings, and we could never make that payment on our own.

> He who did not spare His own Son, but delivered Him up for us all, how shall He not with Him also freely give us all things? (Rom 8:23)

> The next day John saw Jesus coming toward him, and said, 'Behold! The Lamb of God who takes away the sins of the world!' (John 1:29)

> knowing that you were not redeemed with corruptible things, like silver or gold, from your

aimless conduct received by tradition from your fathers, but with the precious blood of Christ, as of a lamb without blemish and without spot (1 Pet 1:18-19)

for even the Son of Man did not come to be served, but to serve, and to give His life a ransom for many. (Mark 10:45)

For Christ also suffered once for sins, the just for the unjust, that He might bring us to God, being put to death in the flesh but made alive by the Spirit. (1 Pet 3:18a)

For God so loved the world that He gave His only begotten Son, that whoever believes in Him should not perish but have everlasting life. For God did not send His Son into the world to condemn the world, but that the world through Him might be saved. He who believes in Him is not condemned; but he who does not believe is condemned already, because he has not believed in the name of the only begotten Son. (John 3:16-18)

Spiritually, you have been forgiven in Christ Jesus. You can see why God makes a big deal of forgiveness. After all, He gave His one and only Son purposefully so you and I can be forgiven. He offered Himself up when we were still sinners (Rom 5:8) and before you were even born. You and I did nothing to deserve His forgiveness, yet He gave it freely.

God wants us to forgive others too, even if they did nothing to deserve it. This can be a difficult concept to accept because I know some readers will have endured horrific events. I pray you find the peace your soul longs for, and that God will reveal what He wants you to do about forgiveness. Please consider the following verses:

For if you forgive men their trespasses, your heavenly Father will also forgive you. But if you do not forgive men their trespasses, neither will your Father forgive your trespasses. (Matt 6:14-15)

But I say to you, love your enemies, bless those who curse you, do good to those who hate you, and pray for those who spitefully use you and persecute you. (Matt 5:44)

And be kind to one another, tenderhearted, forgiving one another, even as God in Christ forgave you. (Eph 4:32)

Pursue peace with all people, and holiness, without which no one will see the Lord; looking carefully lest anyone fall short of the grace of God; lest any root of bitterness springing up cause trouble, and by the many become defiled. (Heb 12:14-15)

Bearing with one another, and forgiving one another, if anyone has a complaint against another, even as Christ forgave you, so you almost must do. (Col 3:13)

You can see an important pattern. God wants you to forgive those who have come against you and wronged you. He wants you to do this, even if you do not know how. I have worked with many, many people who tell me, "Anita, I don't really want to forgive this person, and even if I did, I don't know how!"

God honors all attempts to move closer to His will and His wishes ("Draw near to God and He will draw near to you," James 4:8). This means in any movement toward Him, He will reciprocate and respond. You must come to God with an honest heart, as well as a desire to obey His commands.

For someone who is reluctant to forgive, or maybe you blatantly do not want to forgive a person, simply start by acknowledging your blocks. God knows you have them already. In prayer, tell God, "Lord, you know what this person did to me. I know you want me to forgive him, but I do not want to. Lord, please help me to want to forgive him!"

Be sincere in wanting to please God, while also acknowledging you are far from obedience. Once you start praying regularly in this manner, stay alert for ways in which God communicates back to you. Be open to His nudges, both within your own spirit and from input from other people and outside events. The Lord will answer you in many varied ways, so receive His messages.

If you want to forgive a person, but do not know how to forgive them, again go to God in honest prayer. Here is a suggested prayer: "Lord, I want to forgive her, but I simply do not know how. Can you show me, Lord?" As with the previous prayer, be alert to His prompts. He will guide you toward the forgiveness you desire.

Psychological research indicates that the more time someone spends in trying to forgive someone, the more likely they are to forgive quickly. It is always amusing to me when science "proves" what God has already told us! Because forgiveness is so clearly in His will, it makes sense that He will move the willing heart closer and more rapidly toward forgiveness.

If it helps, the mental health field suggests a few strategies to move toward forgiveness. First, try to see the situation from the offender's point of view. This is referred to as developing empathy. You do not want to make excuses for the offender. But the goal is to see that other person as hurting, flawed, and most likely simply doing the best they are able.

Second, reflect on times when you may have hurt someone. How did you behave? Did you ask for forgiveness? Can you see how vulnerable and fragile we all are? And third, state out loud, "I forgive [person's name]." When you say it out loud, notice how you feel. Have you really forgiven them or do you sense resentment and bitterness? Remember that this is a process and a journey. Allow God to direct and determine this path, being open to His promptings each step of the way.

One last concept around forgiveness is vitally important but often overlooked. You must forgive *yourself.* We have all done things that have either hurt someone else, grieved the Holy Spirit, or hurt yourself. We can know that God forgives us, but for some reason, we continue to hold the offense against ourselves. Perhaps you did something particularly extreme and have asked the Lord to forgive you. But secretly you think, "Well, God may forgive me, but I can never forgive myself because what I did was so bad!"

Please let yourself off the hook. If God forgives you, but you believe what you did was beyond forgiveness, are you implying that God is wrong? Are you a better judge of what should be forgivable than God is? Do you know something more than God knows?

It mocks God's gift to us if we hold offenses against ourselves for which He has already forgiven us. You can rest assured that releasing yourself from resentment directed at yourself is in alignment with God's kingdom. As with all difficulties, if you do not know how to forgive yourself, pray and ask the Lord to show you how.

Repentance

When I fasted for 40 days, I read a wonderful book by Anne Graham Lott entitled, *The Daniel Prayer*. In it, she breaks down the powerful prayer of Daniel, in which he asks God to deliver the nation of Israel out of Babylon and back into their homeland. Daniel begins his prayer with repentance. He acknowledges how God's people have strayed from God's will, and he repents on behalf of the nation. This paved the way for making his profound request of God.

Ms. Lott includes an excerpt from another book listing how we might each, individually, need to repent. I went through many of the topics and found so many areas where I was outside of God's will. They ranged from holding onto unforgiveness to acting in disobedience regarding something I knew God wanted me to do, to not spending more time in His Word.

I never felt condemned in this process but rather convinced by the truth of the light God was shining in my heart. He wanted me to move into alignment with Him and to reject my own ways. I asked Him to speak directly and show me the places I remain distant from His will. This is a humbling exercise, but I knew it to be crucial to my pursuit of Him.

What is biblical repentance? Examining the Hebrew and Greek words used in the original Scriptures, we understand that repentance means to "turn away from evil or to change one's mind with a sense of regret and remorse." Repentance involves far more than simply asking for forgiveness, or even apologizing. It requires an intentional and deliberate move away from sinful, inappropriate, or undesirable behavior. While salvation is not threatened by the lack of repentance, acknowledging our improper behavior with a heartfelt willingness to change puts us in alignment with God. Behavior against God's will takes us off the path He has designed for each of us and diminishes the fruit we can produce in His kingdom.

More than just about anything, I want to reach heaven and hear God say to me, "Well done, good and faithful servant." I want to steward the talents, gifts, and strengths with which He blessed me. I often reflect on the parable of the talents when I consider the issue of repentance. I have a deep sense of responsibility when reading Luke 12:48b: "For everyone to whom much is given, from him much will be required; and to whom much has been committed, of him they will ask the more." I recognize areas in which God has blessed me, and I know He expects me to use those blessings for the advancement of His kingdom. If I get distracted by tasks, thoughts, or issues outside of His will, then I am not meeting this responsibility.

Along with the dereliction of duty, by maintaining an unrepentant heart, I delay His healing. How can He heal me if I remain outside of His will? We know all through Scripture that repentance is clearly important to God. In fact, it is likely one of the most important things to Him, because Jesus began His ministry with the words, "'The time is fulfilled, and the kingdom of God is at hand. Repent, and believe in the gospel" (Mark 1:15).

John the Baptist proclaimed to the Pharisees and Sadducees, "Therefore bear fruits worthy of repentance" (Matt 3:8). Jesus Himself said something very sobering: "but unless you repent you will all likewise perish" (Luke 13:3). In the book of 2 Peter, we are told by one of the apostles who spent three years with Jesus that "the Lord is not slack concerning His promise, as some count slackness, but is longsuffering toward us, not willing that any should perish but that all should come to repentance" (3:9).

There is something about the lack of repentance that results in perishing. Coming to Christ requires acknowledging our sinful nature, the areas we have fallen short and require a savior. But He also wants us to repent. He wants us to realize the ways in which we act contrary to His will and commands, to stop doing those things, and then to turn our eyes to Him and His ways. "Truly, these times of ignorance God overlooked, but now commands all men everywhere to repent" (Acts 17:30).

Please understand that this exercise of asking God where He wants us to change is not about producing guilt! This process of asking God what He wants us to repent of will likely produce what Paul called a "godly sorrow" or "godly grief." He tells us that "godly sorrow produces repentance leading to salvation, not to be regretted; but the sorrow of the world produces death" (2 Cor 7:10). When we become aware of our need to repent, we will experience an emotion that is proper but not consuming or condemning. "As many as I love, I rebuke and chasten. Therefore be zealous and repent" (Rev 3:19). God corrects us, teaches us, and disciplines us. Remember, God is trying to conform us to the image of Christ (Rom 8:29). He does this by correcting us when we act or behave in an unChristlike fashion.

What are you doing that displeases God? In what ways have you ignored His promptings or His commands? Is there an area of your life that you know He wants you to change, to avoid, or to jettison all together, yet you hold on to it? Is there a bad habit, or a way of treating another person, that is less than godly, or are you stingy with your giving and tithes? Do you let bitterness or distrust hinder your relationship? Do you tend to find fault with others? Do you speak behind people's backs? Do you take care of what passes your lips and mind about others? Do you tend to exaggerate in order to be seen or heard, which ends up distorting the truth? Have you become so sensitized to being offensive that you fail to properly apply God's truth to those you know and love?

I tend to judge people in my mind. I have to repent often for being frustrated at drivers on the road or people who post on social media about topics with which I disagree. Of course, repenting for something means that I no longer intend to *do* the thing for which I repent. Therefore, the fact I find myself repeatedly repenting means there is a deeper issue that I need to take to God.

I mention my own issues because I want you to know that you are not alone in having "stuff" to deal with. God knows each of our hearts far better than we know our own, and He knows we are human. This does not absolve us of responsibility, but it gives me comfort to know that as long as I put Him first, and regularly seek His kingdom, His mercies are new every morning (Lam 3:23). As long as I approach repentance with a genuine desire to turn away from the behavior and allow Him to change my heart so that I no longer want to indulge in that behavior, He honors this important gesture. I often remind myself that after healing a few people, Jesus told them to "go and sin no more" (John 5:14; 8:11). Sin harms us, and while Jesus heals, He also does not want us repeating behaviors that create infirmity. He tells us to sin no more because it is in our best interests to avoid sin. He wants repentance because it is good for us and because He loves us.

Free Will

I approach this issue with sensitivity, as I have full awareness that it can seem like "blaming the victim" if not properly examined and understood. We do not knowingly or willfully invite sickness or emotional pain on ourselves. In no way do we "ask for" abuse or bad things to happen to us. We are not beholden to the Hindu notion of karma. Things do happen to us that are entirely out of our control. How we respond to those events, however, is entirely *within* our control.

In his book, *Awakening*, Pastor Stovall Weems says that God is a "filler, not a forcer." In other words, God will not force Himself, including His healing, on anyone. In much the same way that His salvation is ours to claim, God has things set up for us to have a role in healing. We may think, "God knows I'm hurting and He knows what needs to be healed, so why doesn't He just do it?" Sometimes that role means going to the doctor to get an antibiotic. Or you may go to a therapist to seek counseling. Or your role might be to attend your regular physical therapy appointments. In each of these cases, God has empowered the medical profession to provide healing in various ways. But it is up to us to access those modalities. Even if your physical therapist comes to your house to provide a service, you still must do the moves she recommends.

Throughout the Bible, we read stories of Jesus healing people. Over and over again, He heals. In most cases, the person He heals first *does something* to pursue healing. As an example, let us look at Mark 8:22-26.

> Then He came to Bethsaida; and they brought a blind man to Him, and begged Him to touch him. So he took the blind man by the hand and led him out of the town. And when He had spit on his eyes, and put His hands on him, He asked if he saw anything. And he looked up and said, "I see men like trees, walking." Then He put His hands on his eyes again and made him look up. And he was restored and saw everyone clearly. Then He sent him away to his house, saying,

"Neither go into the town, nor tell anyone in the town."

In this story, see how many times Jesus required something of the blind man. The man had to follow Jesus out of town (I assume the man did not know where Jesus was leading him to), then he had to allow Jesus to spit on his eyes. For a moment, consider if the Lord has an unusual or strange way of healing you – are you willing to endure it? There is then a back-and-forth conversation, with Jesus doing something different to the man to restore full sight.

The man had to do things before Jesus would heal him. We do not know why, but it is certainly true: we are to follow Jesus and obey Him. If He is telling us to do something *first*, then we must do it before full healing can be released. In addition, the man and his friends had to approach Jesus. They demonstrated faith in the ability of Jesus to heal him. I believe that our faith, coupled with the healing power of Jesus Christ, is the synergy needed to heal on earth. Our participation is required.

Also, notice the man's healing came in stages. This is so typical of emotional healing as well. The Lord will speak directly to the wounded part of your heart, and He makes it new again. But more of your heart carries wounds and scars. It means we must return to God for more and more healing. Because He did it once, He will do it again. This builds our faith in God, our Heavenly Father! This process of returning for deeper levels of healing causes us to rely more profoundly on the source of all healing, Jehovah Rapha.

So what does this mean? It means that if there is something in your life that you *know* God wants you to do, then holding back on your obedience also holds back your own personal healing. I do not know why God has arranged things in this way, but it is clearly the way things work.

One of the tasks He may be nudging you to do is to trust Him to let down your defenses for the purpose of His healing your heart. Over time, you have built up a defensive wall around your heart. You must allow a crack in that wall to give access to God. Cracking them open can feel painful because it means you are looking full-on at a very upsetting thing you believe about yourself. Maybe you have written on your heart, "I am invisible." Or, "I don't matter." Or, "I am unlovable, dirty, worthless, unimportant."

Confronting, even for a moment, the thing you have been hiding away for your entire life will feel overwhelming. But it is a necessary part of healing. God will not heal what you do not acknowledge. And you will not grow in your relationship with God if there is nothing required from you.

A few years ago, I ended up in the urgent care center because of a kitchen accident. I happen to love acorn squash (I promise this story has a relevant point!). My wonderful husband does not love acorn squash. So occasionally when he is out of town, I will buy a squash for myself to make and enjoy. If you have never prepared an acorn squash, you may not know that it is actually a difficult squash to prepare. The outer shell not only looks exactly like an acorn, but it is very hard to cut through. In fact, you need an extremely sharp knife for the job. Luckily, I have such a knife.

One evening I was cutting the squash to prepare it for dinner. Somehow the knife slipped and ended up cutting into my pinky finger in a rather jagged, deep way. As I looked at it, I knew the pain would come very soon. This is unpleasant for anyone, but for me, it might mean even more trouble. Sometimes when I hurt myself badly, I faint. And then I might even have a seizure. So these troublesome injuries can turn into something more dramatic if I allow it!

Because I know this about myself, I have trained myself to go lay down and put my legs up, forcing more blood to my brain. This helps prevent me from fainting, but it also means I am limited in taking care of myself. In this situation, I needed to get somewhere for stitches. My younger son was home but did not have his driver's license yet. I called him downstairs, told him the situation, and asked him to call my mother to come help. She lives only 15 minutes away, and she is a loving mom. She showed up not more than 20 minutes later and drove me to urgent care.

While all of this was happening, I was on the ground. I wanted to prevent pain, but also, I seriously did not want to *see* the injury. I knew the visual would make me lightheaded. My solution was to put two of my fingers on the injury and apply pressure. This helped control bleeding, pain, and me seeing the jagged, fleshy cut. Not only is this sound first aid, but it also helped my unique personal situation!

We arrived at urgent care and went into the exam room. When the doctor came in, she said, "OK, let's see what we have here." In order for me to let her, the healer, fix my wound, I needed to remove my finger. I had to release the thing that was preventing more problems in order to get the root problem healed. When I took my fingers away, I knew there would be a surge of pain and possibly blood. But that only lasted a small amount of time. Soon enough I got numbing medication, and she stitched me up. Seven stitches and an hour later, I walked out of the urgent care center on the mend.

But notice what I had to do to facilitate the healing. I had developed a strategy – putting pressure with two of my fingers – that held the pain and discomfort off. At a certain point, I had to expose my wound to the one person who could properly manage it. Otherwise, if I had insisted she fix my cut without removing my fingers, she would have said to me, "I'm sorry but I cannot help you if you do not show me your wound."

Emotionally, the same dynamic happens with God and our hurting hearts. We have to show Him our wound before He can speak to it with the healing words that only the Creator of the universe can speak. It means we must allow a crack in that carefully constructed defensive wall around our hearts. It means that, for a moment, we may have to connect with the terribly painful things we wrongly believe about ourselves. But in that moment, we are being still. We are in the *raphah* stillness of acknowledging that we cannot fix our hurts and scars. We hold up the evidence of our battle-wounded soul, submitting it to God Almighty, Jehovah Rapha, the One who declares the end from the beginning. Exposing that hurting heart surrenders to the truth of the omnipotence, omnipresence, and omniscience of our God. We can then ask Him, "Lord, here is what I believe about myself, although I know it is a lie. What do You want me to know about it?"

Keeping those defenses up prevents full healing. Honestly, most people who have trouble letting down their defenses have a major trust problem with God. In fact, I also did not fully trust God. Before He could heal my wounds from anxiety and an overzealous need to control things that I cannot control, He prompted me to admit to myself that I did not trust God to control my life. Until He first set me straight about that, I could not let my wall down even a little.

Do you have this problem? Do you trust God, but only to a certain point? If so, this may be the place for you to pray and ask the

Lord for guidance on how to proceed. It might feel vulnerable to expose yourself, even to God. If so, this is where your free will is interfering with your healing. For God to speak healing words to you, you must let Him. Some readers will have trouble with this concept. Their trust may have been so irreparably betrayed that the thought of even trusting God with their hearts is impossible.

If this is the case, please start where you are with God! He knows exactly what you grapple with, and He stands at the ready to walk with you through whatever path you need to learn to trust Him. "Have I not commanded you? Be strong and of good courage; do not be afraid, nor be dismayed, for the LORD your God is with you wherever you go" (Josh 1:9). "Let not your heart be troubled; you believe in God, believe also in Me" (John 14:1).

You are not alone in your mistrust of God. People admit this to me all the time, and as I have told you, I also did not trust Him enough with my heart at the beginning of my fast. Go to God first with your doubts. Tell Him, with a genuine heart, "Lord, I know I am supposed to trust You, but I do not. Please show me how to trust You!" He will respond, so look for His answer. Then build from there.

The ugly side of free will is that sometimes other people's free will intersects with ours, essentially taking away our free will at a moment in time. People violate us, hurt us, and victimize us because they have the free will to do so. Life is difficult because we all have the ability to heal and to hurt, to elevate and to bring down, to support and to disappoint. Being in Christ does not shield us from these things. Being in Christ gives us the capacity to cope with those things, allowing Him to pick up the pieces and make them right. Abraham acted in his own power, and God had to come along to fix the problem. But his disobedience permeates our global society even to this day.

If Jesus Christ manifested Himself physically in front of you right now, He would have palpable love and power emanating from Him. You would clamor to touch Him so He would heal the thing you want most to be healed. And He would do it because you approached Him and asked Him in faith. We need to pursue Him with that same fervor, with that same intensity, faith, and belief that He will heal the one thing we want most to be made whole.

Our job is to be still.

That *raphah*, healing stillness says to the Lord God Almighty, "I have tried to defend myself for decades to keep my heart safe. And it doesn't work. I chip away, I peel away a tiny part of my defenses to expose my wounded heart to You. I want You to tell me what You say about my wound."

That is what free will looks like. It is trusting God enough to let Him look at your wounded heart and let Him take care of it in His way. We need to let go of trying to do it ourselves. We must stop looking for an answer outside of God. It is time to surrender, submit, be silent, and receive His Word to us.

Chapter Eleven: The Healing Lifestyle

We have done a deep dive into inner healing issues. You learned about how our emotional wounds develop, the role of our spiritual enemy along with the natural reality of living in a fallen world. You learned that it is your heart that is the target of the attacks because it is out of the heart that our thoughts, speech, and actions emerge. When your heart is hurt, it becomes impossible to fully and effectively operate at your highest capacity in God's kingdom.

You learned how very important it is to God that you receive His healing. Mark 1:29-31 tells a story of Jesus going into Simon Peter's house, in which his mother-in-law was sick with a fever. With one touch, Jesus healed that fever and Peter's mother-in-law immediately started serving them. I believe God chose to include this event in Jesus' ministry because it demonstrates the power of healing. What happened when she got better? She was able to serve others. That is what will happen to you. Your healed heart will have a direct and powerful impact on others around you, not to mention God's kingdom at large.

You learned how we all, in our humanness, attempt to manage our wounded hearts on our own. We find ways to make unpleasant feelings go away and to keep ourselves safe. But these strategies either fail to work or they end up causing other problems. Consider what happens when we reach for snack food when we feel down or depressed. Over time, that can have tremendous health impacts. Yet for those moments when we eat, those bad feelings subside.

Most importantly, you learned about the position you can take to receive the inner healing that God has available for you. This position is being still. You learned about how God defines stillness, and that it encompasses much more than physical motionlessness. You read about *raphah* stillness, meaning that you stop striving. You stop trying to fix the problem yourself, you stop searching and yearning. Rather, you stand down, you slacken your efforts and become more like Mary and less like Martha. You put yourself in a reverential state of receiving whatever God has to say as you expose to Him the lies you believe about yourself. Remember, it is these lies that create the wounds on your heart.

From this place of stillness, we can know that He is God. We can acknowledge and receive the truth of His omnipotence, omnipresence, and omniscience. We surrender to the sovereign God of the universe, knowing how limited we are, but that He is limitless. Indeed, He is the One who *created* power. So we can trust in Him to use it for our good.

You now have a list of 10 strategies to use to help you move into the posture of biblical stillness. I hope you try several of them. You will recall that it will probably take some time to "train your brain" to get into this position. Go easy on yourself and allow yourself the time and space to achieve stillness.

You may have been thinking to yourself as you read this book, "Well, this seems great, but I just do not have extended chunks of time to make this happen! Is there any hope for me?"

YES! Of course there is hope! Maybe you are a mom of young children. Maybe you work multiple jobs and "free time" is an illusion. Maybe you take care of a medically ill child or an aging parent and your days are so packed full of obligations that finding any kind of quiet time, let alone extended amounts of quiet time, simply cannot happen.

I completely understand! Short of cutting into your nighttime sleep (which I do not recommend, by the way – adequate sleep is crucially important to good mental and physical health), finding time to be alone with God might feel like a fantasy. In reality, it might be a far-off dream at this point in your life.

But I want to give you hope that you *can hear from God,* no matter how much time you have. The key is finding ways to insert Him into your daily life. That may sound obvious, but perhaps you have not done it yet. If you commute for even ten minutes in the car, turn the radio or music off, and use the silence of the car to talk to God. Allow Him to speak back to you. Over time, you will find yourself becoming more discerning of His voice. You will also feel more comfortable in approaching Him with your biggest hurts and pains.

When you clean your house, do your dishes, fold your laundry, or mow the grass, pray out loud. Have worship music playing in the background to get your mind and spirit more in alignment with Him and then get in the habit of praying to Him. Make sure you leave time to silence yourself with the expectation of hearing His voice in response.

If you currently set aside each morning for prayer and devotions, perhaps schedule a period when you can spend a bit more time. For instance, every Saturday, plan to extend your quiet time by 15 minutes. Use those 15 minutes to pursue stillness from the list of 10 strategies back in chapter nine. Each week, build on what you did the week before. Over a relatively short period, you will have developed a powerful prayer relationship with God that will lead to stillness and healing. If weekly is not an option, then perhaps once a month fit it into a day. Whatever schedule works for you, write it down in your calendar and keep it as you would keep any appointment. This is an appointment with God Himself, so you might be more inclined to keep it!

Your emotional health is paramount. It is worth the inconvenience of scheduling extra time in order to pursue healing. If it helps, please also consider scheduling time with a licensed mental health provider. While you can always take your issues straight to God, He also has empowered certain people to compassionately help others through very challenging circumstances. Indeed, certain conditions are best dealt with in the context of therapy. If you have a traumatic background, including sexual or physical abuse, please do reach out to a licensed therapist. If you have troubling memories, flashbacks of traumatic moments, nightmares, or overall have difficulty addressing and confronting your past, seek professional counseling.

In conjunction with your work with a therapist or counselor, continue to seek God. Continue to work toward *raphah* stillness. All healing originates with Him and comes either via another person, circumstance, a group of people, or directly from Him when we position ourselves in biblical stillness.

Page | 154

I understand some people will be reluctant to make emotional healing a priority. Their history of abuse, neglect, or insufficient family life taught them that they do not matter, that they have no voice, nor any inherent value. None of these beliefs are true. If God put you here, then He makes you worthy in His Son, He says you are His masterpiece, He sees you, your name is written on the palm of His hand, and He loves you with an everlasting love. Learning how to lean into Christ in this way will build your faith as well as heal your heart and soul. It is worth it, although I know it is scary to think about.

I Have Had Healing – Now What?

You have been still, and you have heard a direct, personal, intimate word from the Lord that had the immediate effect of healing a wounded part of your heart. Praise God! This is transformative, and now you can move more boldly in the world, unencumbered by the heaviness of the hurt and pain.

So, what happens now?

Let us turn to John chapter 9 and the story of the man who was blind from birth. This is an incredible miracle. As Jesus walks with His disciples, He sees a man who was born blind. After spitting onto some dirt to make clay, Jesus anoints the man's eyes and then tells him to wash himself off. The man returns from washing himself with his vision fully restored. Hallelujah!

When questioned by the religious authorities, the man says, "Whether He is a sinner *or not* I do not know. One thing I know: that though I was blind, now I see" (John 9:25). What a tremendous statement at both the physical and spiritual level. The comprehensive healing this man experienced must have changed his life forever.

Consider what it must have been like before Jesus Christ came into his life. He would have had an environment that completely supported his blindness. To survive, his parents probably would have kept him in their house, doing things for him that they would not have to do for a son who had his sight. This man would have been limited in his vocation and may not have earned an income. His friends and the community at large probably would have helped him get around and do whatever activities he could perform.

Imagine what happens when, in one instant, this man encounters the God of the universe and his debilitating infirmity is forever destroyed. We learn in the story how his healing actually provokes controversy, and his parents are even forced into a defensive position in front of the authorities who were so off-track that they could not praise the Creator of the heavens and earth for curing a man of his blindness.

What happened to this man the next day when he woke up with fully functioning eyes? His miraculous healing removed a massive barrier in his life. What a blessing! But now what? He would have woken up to the same environment that he had the day before. It would be filled with people, habits, and routines that all existed specifically to manage his blindness. Now that he is no longer blind, he would have been faced with all kind of challenges.

Not only would he have to learn the meaning of colors, and shapes, and the faces of the people he had known his whole life, but he would have to learn how to get along in the world on his own. This undoubtedly took time. Plus, I am certain it would have been a challenge for his parents. I wonder if it was hard for his mother to let him go since she must have been more involved in his life because of the blindness. A mother's instinct to protect could create friction and conflict if she had any reluctance to seeing him explore his independence.

This is the other side of healing. Healing always makes us more whole and increases our faith in the Lord. It also brings new challenges. Your problems will not all disappear with healing. In fact, it often creates new situations that force new types of decisions and behaviors.

Imagine that your wound from childhood that caused you to keep your opinions to yourself and to remain invisible has healing from the Lord. He spoke to you and told you the truth – that He sees you and that you are His. Suddenly, you realize that your opinions, thoughts, preferences, and concerns are just as legitimate as other people's, so you start voicing them. You may have to adjust to the sensation of using your voice because it may feel unnatural, or even weird, at first.

But consider the people around you, in particular those closest to you. They love you and care about you, but they are not used to hearing you voice opinions. It could possibly shock them and even bring up defensiveness. From the healed person's standpoint, everyone should be pleased that she can now speak freely. It can even feel hurtful to experience backlash at speaking from your new healed platform.

You must guard yourself against attempts to bring you back down to a wounded state or to punish you for behaving differently. Some of the backlash you might experience can be mitigated or blunted with good communication. For instance, in this example with the person who now knows that the opinions and thoughts God gave her are worthy of having a voice, she might want to have a conversation about her healing with the important people in her life. It is important that we understand that our healing belongs to us. The people around us have not been privy to what happened to you. All they know is that they could reasonably predict how you would respond and behave, and now they cannot.

Have mercy on them by letting them know what they might expect from you. Admit that for most of your life, for instance, you withheld your opinions and thoughts because you never felt important enough to express them. Now you do know you are a child of God, so that means people around you should expect different things from you.

This mercy you extend to others also is necessary when considering how you speak and behave. If any part of you is angry or resentful about how much you have withheld over the years, you might tend to express your opinions with an edge, or in a more dogmatic way. You may want to pray about asking God to help you not speak in anger but rather out of fact. Say what you want to say, but in a loving, respectful tone. This is especially important if your healing involved learning how to set proper boundaries with others.

As part of leading the healing lifestyle, you will get accustomed to expecting new situations to arise. Sometimes those new situations reveal the next area of your life to take to the Lord for healing. Other times, they deepen relationships. In other cases, you may discover that some relationships are no longer healthy for you. This means learning how to manage that reality with a loving heart.

You can do this. You can learn to be still, according to God's definition, to access healing and wholeness. Surround yourself with people who are trustworthy and know the Bible. Regularly pursue stillness and see how God moves in your heart.

I am confident that you will be forever grateful to Jesus for His work in you! Let me end this book with my prayer for you:

> Lord God, the Maker of heaven and earth, You, the One who knows all things, the One who is the same yesterday, today, and forever, the One who loves this reader with an everlasting love, the One who answers when we call and Who tells us great and mighty things, I lift up this reader to You. You know more about this person's situation than even they know. You know the end from the beginning. You are the reader's strength, shield, redeemer, deliverer, and horn of salvation. In You the reader trusts.

> Lord God, I ask that you show this dear reader how much You love them by gently reminding them of the wound they have on their heart. Let the reader know the lie that is written on their heart. And Lord, as the reader pursues Your stillness, speak to them about what you want them to know.

> Jesus, guard the reader's heart with your peace and power. Be the reader's rearguard; go before them and speak Your truth directly to their hurting heart. Let the reader know what You want them to know. I thank you, Jesus, that you came to bind the brokenhearted and to set the captives free from the prison chains of believing lies. In you, Jesus, we have true freedom and victory, and I claim that for the reader right now, in the MIGHTY name of Jesus Christ, AMEN.